Praise for

Lean Learning

"Better is possible. But it requires focused curiosity and persistence. Flynn's book offers us a useful foundation for growth."

—Seth Godin, author of *This is Strategy*

"Genius! *Lean Learning* streamlines your ability to achieve anything you want and more. Overlearning has stopped you your whole life from doing what you want to do. I've personally watched Pat Flynn's innovative lean learning approach transform his life and business. Pat's principles have changed my life and the lives of countless others who've followed his example. Read *Lean Learning* and watch your life go from info-overload stagnation to action-packed productivity and joy."

—Richie Norton, bestselling author
of *Anti-Time Management*

"*Lean Learning* is the ultimate guide to moving from inspiration to action. Pat Flynn's refreshingly simple strategies teach a new way of consuming information—one that leads to real creation and progress. If you're ready to stop overthinking and start making meaningful moves toward your biggest goals, this book is your roadmap."

—Jenna Kutcher, *New York Times*
bestselling author of *How Are You, Really?*

"Over the years I've watched in awe as Pat dominates practically every endeavor he takes on, from online business, to podcasting to YouTube and much more. Finally in *Lean Learning*, he peels back the curtain and hands you his blueprint for going from inspiration to implementation."

—Allan Dib, author of
The 1-Page Marketing Plan and *Lean Marketing*

"In *Lean Learning*, Pat Flynn reveals a powerful truth: more knowledge isn't the answer—taking action is. Through eye-opening stories, including a preschool class that solved a real-world problem in a single day, Pat introduces a game-changing approach to learning. Instead of getting stuck in overthinking and information overload, he teaches us how to focus on what matters, take action faster, and make real progress—without the overwhelm. If you're ready to stop consuming and start doing, this book will show you how."

—Chris Ducker, bestselling author of
Rise of the Youpreneur and *Virtual Freedom*

"*Lean Learning* isn't just another productivity book—it's a paradigm shift in how we approach personal growth and skill acquisition. I've known Pat Flynn for 12 years and he has created an actionable blueprint for turning inspiration into reality, without getting lost in endless preparation. A must-read for entrepreneurs, professionals, and lifelong learners who are ready to IGNITE!"

—John Lee Dumas, host of *Entrepreneurs on Fire*

"I'm SO TIRED of getting overwhelmed and bogged down by information. How to learn smart, act fast, and succeed turns out to be Pat's real genius. This book is a total gem."

—Michael Bungay Stanier, author of *The Coaching Habit*

"This book is a lifeline. It's the exact blueprint to cut through the noise, trust yourself, and start building the business and life you desire."

—Amy Porterfield, *New York Times*
bestselling author of *Two Weeks Notice*

"Whether you're an entrepreneur, career professional, or someone pursuing a passion project, *Lean Learning* provides the tools to turn your goals into reality. Pat Flynn's authentic approach and real-world examples make this book both inspiring and immediately applicable."

—Lewis Howes, *New York Times* bestselling author
and show host of *The School of Greatness*

"In today's fast-paced world, knowledge is power—but only if it's acquired efficiently and applied effectively. Pat Flynn's *Lean Learning* offers a game-changing approach to cutting through the noise and focusing on high-value learning. As a business and life coach, I've dedicated my career to helping others optimize their performance, and I can say with confidence that this book belongs on the shelf of anyone looking to learn smarter, not harder."

—Michael Hyatt, *New York Times*
bestselling author and business coach

"*Lean Learning* is the real deal. Instead of shortcuts, it gives you a powerful system to master what you NEED to know."

—Chris Guillebeau, author of
The $100 Startup and *Time Anxiety*

Get Free Access to My
Lean Learning Companion Course!

Don't just read about *Lean Learning*—experience it.

As you embark on this *Lean Learning* journey, I've created a free companion course designed to amplify your results at every step.

The companion course seamlessly integrates with each chapter, providing:

- Guided explanations that bring key concepts to life
- Implementation strategies for your specific challenges
- A behind-the-scenes look at key principles of *Lean Learning* in action

Also, each chapter references specific resources available in the course—exactly when you need them—so you can immediately apply what you're learning without getting overwhelmed.

Think of it as having me right beside you as you progress through the book—clarifying concepts, answering questions, and helping you adapt these methods to your unique situation.

Visit leanlearningbook.com/course to get immediate access.

Let's do this!

Lean Learning

How to Achieve More by Learning Less

Pat Flynn

Simon Acumen

New York   Amsterdam/Antwerp   London

Toronto   Sydney/Melbourne   New Delhi

SIMON
ACUMEN

An Imprint of Simon & Schuster, LLC
1230 Avenue of the Americas
New York, NY 10020

First Simon Acumen hardcover edition June 2025

SIMON ACUMEN is a trademark of Simon & Schuster, LLC

Simon & Schuster strongly believes in freedom of expression and stands against censorship in all its forms. For more information, visit BooksBelong.com.

For information about special discounts for bulk purchases, please contact Simon & Schuster Special Sales at 1-866-506-1949 or business@simonandschuster.com.

The Simon & Schuster Speakers Bureau can bring authors to your live event. For more information or to book an event, contact the Simon & Schuster Speakers Bureau at 1-866-248-3049 or visit our website at www.simonspeakers.com.

Interior design by Laura Levatino

Manufactured in the United States of America

10 9 8 7 6 5 4 3 2 1

Library of Congress Cataloging-in-Publication Data has been applied for.

ISBN 978-1-6680-2764-6
ISBN 978-1-6680-2765-3 (ebook)

To my children, as you stand on the threshold of adulthood, may the lessons in these pages guide you to learn with purpose, live with passion, and lead with integrity.

Contents

Introduction

You Know Too Much

"It ain't what you don't know that gets you into trouble. It's
what you know for sure that just ain't so."

— Mark Twain

Jennifer took a deep breath as she looked at the whiteboard
covered in square sticky notes, each inscribed with a word or
two. In the room, sixteen junior design engineers sat brainstorm-
ing solutions to an emergency that had just derailed their day.

For the next hour, she facilitated an intense discussion
with the group, navigating an ocean of ideas on the board. The
goal was simple: narrow the vision to a single solution, create a
prototype, then iterate until the problem was solved.

With such a large and inexperienced group, the task wasn't
easy. But this was the kind of challenge Jennifer had been trained
for. She was ready to guide these young engineers through a process of thinking that would hopefully lead to a productive outcome.

I wasn't in the room that day, but I saw the final product and
it was incredible. The result was beyond anyone's expectation,
and the team was extremely proud of their work.

For myself, and the other outsiders who witnessed the result, we had seen firsthand the power of innovation at work and what a small group of individuals working together can accomplish in a short period of time.

But by far, the most impressive part of the project was that no one on the engineering team was older than five.

Relearning Learning

Jennifer Vasilis (aka Ms. Jenny) was my son's preschool teacher. One day after a massive ant infestation forced the students to eat outside in the hot California sun, Ms. Jenny paused the afternoon's activities to teach her class an important lesson.

Together, they brainstormed about what to do. As the kids shouted out their ideas, Ms. Jenny wrote them down on sticky notes and placed them on the whiteboard. Some ideas were impractical, like eating at Chick-fil-A every day, and others were more bizarre, like just eating the ants for lunch. All ideas were welcome with no filters or fears of judgment, which is a sense of freedom we tend to lose as we grow older. After a bit of time, Ms. Jenny steered the discussion toward a consensus: constructing a sun shade.

I was made aware of this plan in an email Ms. Jenny sent the parents that evening calling for donations of old blankets, PVC piping, and other materials, and during drop-off the next morning, a giant pile of goods was accumulating just outside the preschool door. I wasn't sure what to expect, but when I arrived for pickup later that day, my wife and I, along with several other parents, were in awe of what was standing before us.

On the edge of the concrete courtyard, right next to a small playground, stood two eight-foot-tall banners made of blankets that spanned about six to eight feet wide. The framing was made of PVC pipe that was put together with duct tape, and the feet were weighed down by bags of sand. During lunch that day, the shades were moved next to the tiny lunch tables to block the sun and allow the kids to eat more comfortably outside, and the coolest thing about all this (pun intended) is that the kids built the entire thing themselves.

As the parents were taking pictures, I noticed that the sun shades kind of resembled those "step and repeat" backdrops you see at events where celebrities pose for photographers, except today the celebrities weren't movie stars or musicians, they were these little builders.

How did a group of children build that—in a *day*? They didn't do it by falling into the common traps many adults face when tackling challenges. I don't know about you, but I've seen my fair share of folks felled by overthinking and overanalyzing, spending more time searching for the perfect solution than taking action. At one point or another, we all do it. We create committees and bring in experts to debate the best approach.

Or, more commonly: we find ourselves endlessly consuming more content—downloading the latest podcasts, watching the newest videos, reading the most recent articles—all in the hope that one of these will provide the elusive answer we are seeking. While these resources can be valuable, they more often than not lead to information overload and overthinking, causing us to delay making the simple decisions that would help move us forward.

In contrast, my son's preschool class began their process with a clear problem, then carved out dedicated time in their schedule to address it, and they dove right in and got to work. The children weren't paralyzed by their need for absolute certainty—they were willing to experiment and learn as they went. They didn't feel the need to know everything about sun shades or construction before beginning—they only needed to know enough to get started. They, like the rest of us, could figure out the rest along the way.

This is a valuable lesson for all of us, regardless of age. We all can begin solving our most pressing problems now. We can take those first steps toward something we're inspired to do right away. Today. You don't have to wait. It won't be perfect, but it will be progress.

As a parent watching what was unfolding that day in my kid's classroom, I couldn't help but marvel at the impact this experience must have had on my son and his classmates. To collaboratively brainstorm solutions to a real-life problem, then bring one of those ideas to life in such a short time span, is an incredibly powerful lesson for young minds, one that is sure to shape their approach to future challenges throughout the rest of their lives. This reminded me of my own learning experiences. Like most people, I grew up believing that information by itself was valuable. In fact, my entire high school and college experience was predicated on the idea that the more you knew about more things, the more successful you would become.

Confessions of an Over-Learner

Before we get too far, let me give you a little background on myself. Hi, I'm Pat, and I am an over-learner.

Everyone else: Hi Pat.

My whole life, I have strived to gather as much information as possible so that I could use it somewhere else later. While other people collected Pokémon cards (that would come later), I collected information, and for a long time, this worked well . . . until it didn't.

Working hard and overachieving has always been something that came naturally to me. I worked tirelessly to earn a 4.2 GPA in high school and then graduate magna cum laude from UC Berkeley. But in 2008, just a few years after graduating architecture school, I was laid off from my dream job as an architect during the Great Recession, and none of those things mattered anymore. Nobody was hiring so I couldn't get a job, so I moved back home to San Diego to live with my parents, which was not exactly on my vision board. I knew a lot about architecture, but there I was, twenty-five years old staring at the ceiling of my childhood bedroom, crying out of frustration.

Information had failed me.

On my bedroom wall, next to the Blink-182 and Padres stickers I placed there years ago, were all of my awards and achievements that my parents had framed and displayed. At that moment, I realized all the knowledge I had accumulated, while valuable, had not prepared me for the challenges I now faced.

It was a humbling moment, one that forced me to confront the limitations of my education and the need for a different approach to learning and problem-solving. Little did I know that this painful experience would become the catalyst for a transformative journey of self-discovery and growth, one that would lead me to question the very foundations of what it meant to learn and succeed in an ever-changing world.

On my mission to figure out what to do next to get back on my feet, I quickly fell back into old habits, hoarding information as if it were a drug. I found myself compulsively collecting every scrap of knowledge, addicted to the rush it provided, yet without any clear plan for its application. Every magazine, every book, every blog post and forum I subscribed to made me feel like I was getting somewhere thinking that the more I learned, the better equipped I would be. But in the end, I found myself right back where I started, lying on my bed, overwhelmed, and confused.

It took some time to realize that the problem wasn't a lack of knowledge, but rather the way I had been conditioned to learn. Like many of us, I had been trained to read textbooks, take tests, and regurgitate answers instead of truly understanding what was required to acquire a new skill.

As adults, we tend to repeat this process, getting excited about learning something new, finding resources, applying some effort, then "failing" when we don't see immediate results. This leads to self-doubt and giving up when things get too difficult.

As we navigate through an era marked by swift changes and endless choices, the ability to adapt quickly has never been more crucial. The rise of artificial intelligence and the relentless expansion of digital information have transformed how we all live and work, requiring a shift in how we acquire and apply knowledge.

This moment in time demands more than just traditional learning methods. It demands a strategy that is as fluid and proactive as the rapidly evolving world around us. We don't need more information or another textbook. What we need is a disciplined process to learn the right information at the right time so that we can solve the right problems.

This is what I call "Lean Learning."

Lean Learning is about going back to basics and learning as children do. To solve most problems, you don't need to know everything about a given topic. You don't need to explore every outcome. All you need is the minimum knowledge needed to solve that problem, a willingness to put the information into action, and the resilience to keep going when things get tough. And if a group of five-year-olds can do it, then we can, too.

Embracing Lean Learning has transformed my life in ways I never thought possible. In 2008, I launched my first business, helping architects pass an exam. Since then, I've created several more businesses, invented physical products, started software companies, authored best-selling books, and now serve on the board of several companies and start-ups in the creator economy. I've also cofounded a community of thousands of entrepreneurs who are helping each other on their unique entrepreneurial journey.

But my success is not unique. The principles of Lean Learning have the power to transform anyone's life, regardless of their background or circumstances.

In this book, I'll share with you the strategies and mindset shifts that have helped me and countless others learn faster, solve problems more effectively, and create the lives we desire. It's time to question the way we've been taught to learn and embrace a new approach, one that empowers us to adapt and thrive in an ever-changing world.

In our quest for personal growth and success, however, we inevitably face an unexpected and ironic challenge: the sheer abundance of information available to us.

The End of the Know-it-all

Growing up a latchkey kid, I used to come home every day after school, let myself in, and camp out in my parents' bedroom until they got home from work. They had the better TV.

After dropping a Pop-Tart into the toaster, I'd switch on the square television set, munch on my less-than-healthy snack, and settle in for a nice afternoon of *Saved by the Bell*. When my dad came home from work a few hours later, we'd switch to watching his favorite program: *Jeopardy!*

He'd be lying in bed, tired after a long day of work, and I'd be sitting on the floor looking up at the TV. I remember feeling jealous that the contestants knew most of the answers. I didn't understand a lot of the categories, but on the off chance I'd get a question right, I'd jump for joy. Even back then, I remember how gratifying it felt to know that I knew something random.

Learning things and knowing things can be fun. Attend a

trivia night at any local bar, and you'll find a group of individuals who love to compete on who knows the most about as many topics as possible. Knowing random bits of knowledge can be fun and interesting, but is it all that useful as we try to navigate the complexities of modern life, advance in our careers, or solve real-world problems?

Before the internet, knowledge was a precious commodity. Those who possessed it held a certain power—there was real value in knowing things that others did not. You were more useful and more admired.

For example, if you happened to own an A-to-Z collection of *Encyclopaedia Britannica* in your home, you were likely upper-class. And if you owned two sets (one for downstairs and one for upstairs), then you probably had royalty in your bloodline. Or at least, that's what it seemed like to the rest of us.

Today, however, information is no longer scarce. It's everywhere, all of the time, accessible to everyone with a device. It's like an endless all-you-can-eat buffet of knowledge, available 24/7, and we're all consuming way too much without realizing it. In many cases, it's being forced down our throats.

This is a problem. How we consume content affects everything we do from how we treat our neighbors to how well we perform at our jobs to what kind of parent or spouse we ultimately become. Information really can change your life when you use it, but we can waste a lot of time when you just keep consuming.

Of course, there's no shortage of studies illustrating how technology use and a person's mental health are related. We all understand that too much technology is not good for us, particularly when it comes to the excesses of screen time, the pervasive influence of social media, and the subtle intrusions of AI into our daily lives. Each of these aspects can isolate us, diminish our real-world interactions, and it leaves us distracted and less present in our own lives. What you *won't* find is a piece of research that says unrestricted access to the internet, screens, and social media is good for you. We know how bad it is. We just don't do anything about it. And that needs to change.[1]

Here's the big question, though. If information were the key to success and happiness, then why do some people struggle to achieve their goals despite having access to a wealth of knowledge?

The truth is that it's not just about having the answers or the information; it's about what we do with it. The implementation. **Action without information is chaos, but information without action is a waste.** The key to unlocking our full potential lies in finding the perfect balance between the two.

When we're driven to start something new, the answers are out there, but it can be overwhelming to know where to begin and when to stop. How much information is enough to make a decision? Who can we trust? What about conflicting or outdated information?

And let's not forget about the algorithms that are constantly shaping and curating the information we see, pushing it our way even when we didn't necessarily ask for it. These algorithms are designed to keep us engaged on their platforms longer, prioritizing content that confirms our existing beliefs rather than providing the most accurate or novel information. It's actually harder for us to find truly useful and varied information, and it's a complex and evolving landscape that requires a new set of skills and strategies to navigate effectively.

Lean Learning is the key to building a life of your dreams, one where nearly anything is possible. I know that's a big promise, but it's true in my experience. And if you could become better at more things, more often, what could that make possible?

That's the question I want to answer with this book.

How Lean Learning Works

Lean Learning goes beyond traditional learning—it's about applying what we learn in real time and constantly adapting to enhance our growth. Tailored for a world that constantly disrupts our focus, the essence of Lean Learning is captured in its simplicity and its efficacy.

It is structured around four essential steps:

1. **Identify** what you want to accomplish next.
2. **Learn** only what you need to move forward.
3. **Implement** what you've learned.
4. **Review and repeat** to refine the process to deepen understanding and skill.

At first glance, this may appear deceptively simple, perhaps even insufficient for substantial learning. If you're wondering "What else do I need to do?" that is a normal reflex, and you've also proven my point.

We've been conditioned to equate complexity with value, which drives us straight into the trap of overcomplicating learning. But in Lean Learning, we focus on efficiency—doing just enough to move forward effectively, without getting bogged down by unnecessary details. Trust the process, take it one step at a time, and you'll discover that real power lies in simplicity and action. Here's how each chapter of the book maps to crucial phases of the process:

In Chapter 1, we address the common problem of **inspiration overload** and explore, instead, the art of **selective curiosity.** When we understand how to filter through the noise of endless information and focus on what ignites our curiosity and passion, we truly begin our Lean Learning journeys.

In Chapter 2, we talk about the importance of choosing **action over information.** This is easy to say, harder to do. It's a process that takes time and practice but is totally worth it. When we shift from passive consumption to active application, real learning begins.

In Chapter 3, I share my secret weapon for success. In this chapter, we'll identify the key **champions** every learner needs to make their learning journey a success. Surrounding yourself with mentors, coaches, and a community of supporters marks the critical difference between you reaching your goals and fizzling out too quickly.

In Chapter 4, I will reveal how to **protect your progress.** In this chapter, you'll discover strategies to shield your learning journey from distractions and setbacks, ensuring continuous progress. We all get sidetracked on occasion, and this part of the process will help you know what to do when that happens so that you can keep going.

In Chapter 5, we explore what I call **Voluntary Force Functions.** This is where you implement challenges by choice, using structured pressure to catalyze growth and accelerate skill acquisition. In layman's terms, you put yourself in a position that forces you to do a thing you don't want to do but will ultimately benefit you. It's not *always* fun, but the more you do it, the better you get. And the results will speak for themselves.

In Chapter 6, we address the age-old question in any challenging endeavor: When do you keep going, and when do you change course? **Persist or pivot?** Through regular assessment and honest reflection, we gain a deeper understanding of our progress, or lack thereof, and then make the necessary adjustments to get the most out of our time and effort. The last thing we want to do is keep pushing on a pull door, because we all know how that ends up looking.

In Chapter 7, we tackle the confusing topic of mastery and why it's not always what most people tend to think. In this chapter on **Micro Mastery**, we will focus on making small, consistent gains that add up over time, while also being open to significant leaps—what I call **Quantum Leaps**—that can take place through bolder moves. This is the chapter where you figure out where to focus your efforts and how to go deep even in Lean Learning—which is never about staying in the shallows, just about getting the most return for your investment of effort.

In Chapter 8, we take everything you've learned thus far and make the **transition from learning to leading.** Many think of teaching as something you do after you learn a skill, but I want to argue that teaching is as much a part of the learning process as anything. It's only when we can turn around and share a skill with someone else that we can say we've really learned it. Teaching is an important and critical way to reinforce our learning, helping us consolidate what we know, and offering more value to those around us.

Each chapter not only delves deeper into these steps but also provides you with practical exercises, inspiring stories, and essential lessons to enhance your learning journey.

This book isn't just about acquiring knowledge—it's about transforming that knowledge into wisdom and action. Prepare to unlearn outdated approaches and embrace a streamlined path to personal and professional growth.

Why Lean Learning Matters

In a world where things are constantly changing, the need to stay relevant is greater than ever. But in this ever-changing landscape of increasing technology and connectivity, there lies a hidden opportunity. Instead of getting bogged down by all the content that wants to consume *us*, we can instead put it to good use.

Any skill you want to learn, any skill at all—from ice sculpting to home gardening to learning to code—is now, literally, at your fingertips. Anything you want to do, any idea you have, is accessible. With Lean Learning, you can grab hold of these opportunities and put them to good use. It sounds a little too good to be true, but it's not. In this new world of learning, there is nothing you can't do (seriously).

Inspired by Ms. Jenny's class and others I've met on my own journey, I no longer get bogged down with too much information and too much action. I've learned to take small but consistent actions that lead to massive results. I've learned *this* is the secret to mastering any skill, any field, any area of interest or subject of study.

Most people think it takes thousands of hours—or an entire lifetime—to become an expert. But the truth is that mastery is just the process of taking the next right step at just the right time and letting those small wins build. Because that's what leads to the next opportunity where you'll learn even more, and the one after that, and the next—and so on. Combine these moments, along with the cumulative lessons they provide, and you create a process that helps you continually improve at any skill until you become proficient, then excellent, and ultimately a master.

I want to offer this process to you, this new way of learning that we'll cover in this book, where we solve the problems in front of us instead of the ones we might have . . . *someday*. It's changed my life, and I believe it can change yours, as well.

Adopting the mindset of a Lean Learner will make you happier, feel more useful, and be more successful in any area of life. Everyone thrives when they feel that their lives are connected to a deeper and more meaningful purpose—we can't help it. As Viktor Frankl once captured perfectly in *Man's Search for Meaning*: "Life is never made unbearable by circumstances, but only by lack of meaning and purpose." When we bounce back and forth from one hobby to the next, tackling yet another new idea that we never complete, our lives feel vague and meaningless. But when we dedicate ourselves to a single pursuit and can see ourselves improve, everything changes.

Lean Learning equips us with the skills that not only make us valuable but also ensure our lives are imbued with purpose. It's not just about speeding up the learning process—it's about enriching our lives with purpose and meaning, getting us to that feeling, and reality, of a purposeful life faster.

I don't expect the whole world to change from reading one book, of course, but I do think how we tackle all this information must change. Everything in our world is becoming faster, more complex, and increasingly difficult to manage. With anxiety and depression rates climbing and a general sense of being overwhelmed at an all-time high, it's clear that we need a way to handle the flood of content that never stops coming.

This book offers a method not just for coping but for thriving amid these challenges by focusing on solving the real, pressing problems of today—not just the hypothetical ones of tomorrow. I hope you implement what you learn here. You may discover, as I have, that what you know is only as valuable as the action you take to support your knowledge.

I also hope you pass on some of the lessons you learn. Because these days, we are not just learners—we are teachers and influencers and champions of causes. Or at least, we *can* be. Whether you're an entrepreneur, teacher, manager, parent, or friend, you have the chance to make a difference. And I hope you do.

Speaking of making a difference, the motivational speaker Les Brown once said, "The graveyard is the richest place on earth, because it is here that you will find all the hopes and dreams that were never fulfilled, the books that were never written, the songs that were never sung, the inventions that were never shared, the cures that were never discovered, all because someone was too afraid." But I've often wondered: What if that weren't the case? What if we *weren't* too afraid?

What if we used the knowledge we had to make the greatest impact possible?

What if we put the skills we already had to better use?

What if we didn't doubt ourselves?

If you and I could relearn *how* we learned, more dreams—I believe—would be fulfilled. More books would be written. More songs would be sung. More inventions would be made. The world would become, in short, a much better place in no time at all. It would have to. That's why this book exists. That's why I believe in Lean Learning. If you apply this, it can turn your own world upside down, in the best way possible.

But before we change the world, we first have to change ourselves. And that starts with something simple, something each of us knows intimately: *ourselves*. How do we move from being constantly inspired but never taking action to making a real difference in our own lives as well as in the lives of others? We have to get clear on our purpose, on what we want to accomplish, and what we are willing to commit to.

Lean Learning starts with being selectively curious.

1.

Inspiration Overload
and the Art of Selective Curiosity

"I have no special talents. I am only passionately curious."
— Albert Einstein

Inspiration is wonderfully unpredictable. It can strike at any moment, in any form. Sometimes it's external, like when you're idly scrolling through Instagram and a post catches your eye. Or when your favorite song plays and suddenly, everything clicks.

Other times, it's internal, emerging in those rare, quiet moments when you pause the daily hustle and allow yourself to dream big.

And occasionally, inspiration hits by accident, like when Doc Brown slips, hits his head on the bathroom sink, and has a vision for the flux capacitor—the device that makes time travel (and my all-time favorite movie, *Back to the Future*) possible.

While inspiration can be a powerful motivator, it also has the potential to overwhelm. In today's world, not only are we inundated with information, but we're also constantly exposed to numerous inspiring ideas, each pulling us in different directions. This barrage can lead to an "inspiration overload" where the abundance of potentially transformative sparks makes it difficult to decide which path to pursue.

By the end of this chapter, you will not only master the art of managing inspiration overload but also leave equipped with a definitive action plan on how to tackle it. You'll know precisely which inspirations are worth your time and effort and how to strategically channel your energies into them.

Prepare to transform the chaos of endless possibilities into a focused roadmap that guides your decisions and enhances your creative journey.

Magic

When I was seven years old, I watched my mom cook Filipino food like it was a magic show. My mom, the magician, would somehow take random ingredients, put them into a pot on the stove, and after adding some magic dust, voilà—a delicious soup she called *sinigang*.

Later, I discovered that the "magic dust" she was using was actually tamarind powder, but that doesn't take away from just how mind-blowingly tasteful this dish was, especially when combined with a bowl of rice.

It really was like magic. Like any seven-year-old who watches magic happen before their eyes, I wanted to know how to do it, too.

I didn't waste any time.

I'll spare you the exact details of what happened next, but I ended up making a giant mess. When my parents caught me, I had already coated our kitchen counters with flour, used every mixing bowl in the house, and for some reason had raw ground beef both on the floor and in my mouth. I'm sure it was a sight to behold.

Luckily, I survived. I didn't know you weren't supposed to do that. After my parents taught me about new words like salmonella and E. coli, I eventually got around to asking them, "Can you teach me how to cook?"

I didn't know it at the time, but that initial spark of inspiration—and the messy experiments that followed—helped me develop a skill that nourishes me to this day . Cooking brings me endless joy, especially when I get to share it with others.

My chef "come-up story" was a result of **passion-driven inspiration**, a genuine curiosity that propelled me into the kitchen with an eager desire to re-create the magic I saw.

This initial spark of enthusiasm is typical of passion-driven pursuits, where our deepest interests push us into experiences headfirst. However, as with any endeavor, there are both pros and cons to pursuits driven by such internal motivation.

As children, we have the freedom to explore our curiosity with virtually no boundaries. We have time to try things—like playing different sports, learning musical instruments, and experimenting with science. Some of those experiments evolve into lifelong skills and passions that become part of our identity. Others fade away. But each contributes to the tapestry of our personal growth.

Benefits of Passion-Driven Inspiration

High Engagement	Just as my early experiments in the kitchen were fueled by my fascination with cooking, passion-driven activities often involve a high level of personal engagement and enjoyment. This natural enthusiasm makes the learning process deeply rewarding and intensely personal.
Sustained Interest	Passion keeps us coming back, helping to sustain our interest over time. My ongoing journey with cooking is a testament to how a single moment of inspiration can evolve into a lifelong pursuit of growth, experimentation, and reward.
Personal Fulfillment	Following my passion for cooking has not only enhanced my skills over time, but has also brought me tremendous joy and satisfaction, aligning with my personal values and enriching my life.

Challenges of Passion-Driven Inspiration

Resource Allocation	Balancing this passion with responsibilities such as school, work, or family can be challenging. The time and resources required for such pursuits might sometimes stretch my capabilities and availability.
Practicality	While following passions can lead to personal growth, they don't always align perfectly with practical needs or immediate benefits. It's crucial to weigh the joy against the utility, especially when time is a constraint.
A Bias Toward Comfort	There is a risk of becoming too comfortable within areas we are passionate about, potentially missing out on opportunities to grow in other challenging but beneficial areas.

As adults, however, our reality shifts dramatically. We juggle responsibilities, careers, and family obligations. Our time is limited, and constant stimulation from our surroundings does nothing but scatter our focus. We can no longer afford to explore every fleeting interest. If we want to grow, explore new paths, and try new things, we need to be selective, choosing pathways that align with our responsibilities and enhance our lives.

Other times, however, we don't have a choice, and the need to learn something new is no longer based on passion but rather, necessity.

Mission

If you were to ask me what date changed my life forever, I'd tell you it was the first date I went on with my wife. Then, after you finish rolling your eyes, I'd share this one:

June 17, 2008.

It was a Tuesday morning like any other, and as I entered the architectural office and sat down at my desk, I glanced at the calendar pinned on my cubicle and saw I had golf scheduled for that weekend—something exciting to look forward to, which motivated me to work extra hard that week. But within an hour after my arrival to the office, everything would change.

My boss had called me into his office and shared the bad news: I was getting laid off.

The day I was let go was unlike any other. I walked into the office with a plan for my day, my week, and my future. And an hour later, it all vanished. One moment I had a job, and then the next, *poof*—it was gone. It wasn't magic. It was a harsh reality. I soon found myself on the phone calling every contact in my Rolodex (yes, I had a Rolodex back then), desperate to find any job openings.

But it was too late. The Great Recession had already begun, and there were no job openings. Out of necessity, a new kind of inspiration was about to take hold in my life. This is what sparked a necessity-driven inspiration, one that compelled me to transform my urgent need into a thriving new venture.

In short, losing my job forced me to reassess everything. There was no magic dust, only the pressing need to figure out the next steps—not just for me, but for my family's future. The urgency to create a new path led me to the world of online business, a realm I knew little about but was driven to figure out. It was a harrowing journey but one that ultimately worked out.

If you've been with me on this journey for a while (following via my podcast, website, and social media), then you know the details of those early days. But if not, suffice to say that it was all a challenging mess. Especially in those early days of entrepreneurship.

My first attempts to build a business were littered with mistakes. However, through trial and error and the Lean Learning method I will unpeel for you in this book, I didn't just survive my layoff. I *thrived* because of it. I didn't know it at the time, but the necessity to figure things out had given me the skill to earn millions of dollars across several businesses and serve millions of people all over the world for many years to come.

This period of necessity-driven inspiration taught me an

invaluable lesson: when pushed out of our comfort zones, we can discover untapped reservoirs of potential. It's not about the challenges that come our way but rather how we respond to them that ultimately defines our path in life. This is why necessity-driven inspiration, even when it is forced upon us, should be part of our strategy for growth.

Benefits of Necessity-Driven Inspiration	
Immediate Application	The skills and knowledge I acquired were immediately put to use, ensuring that learning was timely and directly linked to real-world needs.
Problem-Solving Focus	This type of inspiration demands practical solutions, honing my ability to think critically and solve problems on the fly.
Resilience Building	Each challenge overcome in the early days of my entrepreneurial journey reinforced my resilience, teaching me to adapt and persevere despite setbacks.

Challenges of Necessity-Driven Inspiration	
High Pressure	The stakes were high, and the pressure to succeed was intense, often leading to stress and anxiety.
Steep Learning Curve	Without the luxury of leisurely exploring interests, I had to learn new skills quickly, sometimes leading to overwhelming and exhausting experiences.
Risk of Burnout	Prolonged periods of necessity-driven learning and problem-solving can lead to burnout, especially without the intrinsic enjoyment that passion-driven activities provide.

Now, as we navigate the diverse inspirations in our lives, from the magical to the mandatory, how do we manage them effectively? How do we ensure that each spark, whether born from passion or necessity, is given the right attention and placed on the right path?

Enter the "Inspiration Matrix," which we'll cover in detail next. This tool is designed to help you categorize your inspirations into manageable segments, allowing you to prioritize and act on them with clarity and purpose.

Whether you are driven by passion or propelled by necessity, this matrix helps you to see where each inspiration should lead, ensuring that none are lost and all are harnessed to their fullest potential. And perhaps even more useful, you'll begin to learn how to see an inspiration that's not worth your time, and move past it to make room for something more meaningful.

In the following sections, we'll explore how to use the Inspiration Matrix to balance these types of inspirations, helping you convert each into actionable steps that align with your goals and life circumstances.

The Inspiration Matrix

Inspiration, whether fueled by passion or pressed upon us by necessity, comes in many forms. It's essential to know not just how to capture that inspiration but also what to do with it. That's where the Inspiration Matrix comes in: a tool to help us sort these sparks and use them to our advantage.

Take a look at the matrix below:

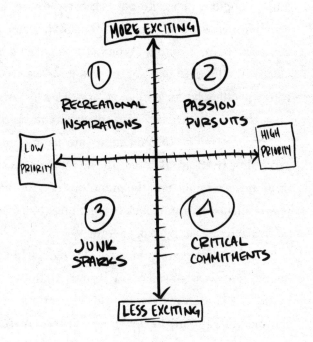

Every idea and inspiration you have can be funneled into this matrix. Like a filter, it will help you understand and make decisions about where to direct (or redirect) your limited time and energy.

Try it for yourself. Think of an idea or inspiration that you've recently had, and then read through the descriptions of each section below.

1. Recreational Inspirations

If you find inspiration nestled within this quadrant, you've identified something that can sprinkle extra joy into your life. These are the pursuits you turn to after a long day or week—not because they are urgent, but because they provide a burst of happiness and a break from routine. Whether it's engaging in creative hobbies, embarking on spontaneous road trips, spending hours gardening, or getting lost in a book, these activities can reset and refresh your spirit.

For me, my go-to recreations are fishing and gardening. Getting out in nature and taking a break from devices, email, and the monotony of a routine is what helps me come back to the things I have to do with a renewed sense of energy.

I started gardening in 2020 during the pandemic, and was considered a "brown thumb." As in, I didn't know anything. But this recreational inspiration allowed me to slow down, distract myself from the craziness of the world, and actually get good at growing food. I still practice it to this day and include getting out into the garden as part of my weekly ritual.

It's crucial to navigate this quadrant with mindfulness. While a rich array of recreational inspirations can signify a full life, spreading yourself too thin can lead to only scratching the surface on each. The key is to dive deeper rather than wider, cultivating a select few activities that truly enrich your life without causing overwhelm.

Everyone is different, of course, but in my experience, maintaining one or two primary recreational pursuits provides the perfect balance. This allows for deep, fulfilling engagement and prevents the dilution of your energies. Remember, life is long and interests can evolve. Dedicating a year or two to diving deep into a few activities can significantly enrich your life, but there's no need to feel locked in forever.

Periodically asking yourself "Does this activity still bring me joy and relaxation?" can help you gauge whether it continues to fit into this category or if it's time to explore new avenues. But by focusing deeply on just a few recreational activities at once, you not only gain more from them but allow yourself the space to grow and evolve within each activity, enhancing your life's tapestry over time.

Embracing these inspirations is not a luxury—it's a critical component of a well-rounded life. These activities might not propel you to your next career milestone, but they play a vital role in maintaining balance, preventing burnout, and fostering well-being. You may not be great (at first), but these are the activities that keep life vibrant and ensure your journey isn't just about the destination but about savoring the moments along the way.

Later, we'll explore strategies for balancing and deepening your engagement with your recreational inspirations. We'll also learn how to integrate these activities into our lives efficiently, ensuring they complement rather than complicate our pursuit of success in more pressing areas. But for now, just know that these are an important part of life and essential to Lean Learning.

2. Passion Pursuits

These pursuits are the beating heart of your ambition. They are the projects and ideas that don't just spark interest—they ignite a bonfire.

These pursuits align deeply with your passions and purpose, resonating with the very core of who you are and what you stand for. This is the work that doesn't feel like work, the projects that have you losing track of time, the creations that have you leaping out of bed in the morning, eager to continue where you left off.

For me, this was the SwitchPod, an idea I had for an invention in 2017. I wanted to change something that was a problem for videographers. I got the bug and needed a solution to the same problem I was having (more about that later). What eventually led to a six-figure product launch started with a simple idea, with a problem—a curiosity. Both my cofounder, Caleb, and I had no idea what we were doing, but we were passionate about something we wanted to fix, and that was enough to begin. This passion of ours eventually led to a business that fulfilled us both deeply and changed our lives in profound ways.

Investing in your Passion Pursuits is not only recommended—it's vital. These pursuits hold the promise not only of personal fulfillment but also the potential for significant achievements that can create a ripple effect on the world around you.

Passion Pursuits can present certain challenges that need to be navigated carefully. While it's okay to have multiple interests, having fewer passions you can focus more deeply on narrows the scope of learning requirements, protects your time, and speeds up the acquisition of new skills.

Later, we'll explore strategies that enable you to give your passions the attention they deserve, while still keeping an eye on the myriad of life's other demands. Finding harmony between your passions and your responsibilities is an art form in itself, one that I look forward to helping you master.

3. Junk Sparks

Not every shiny object is worth your attention. Junk Sparks are fleeting distractions that offer little value and can significantly sidetrack you from your goals. These distractions may glimmer with promise, but upon closer examination, they usually fail to provide a long-lasting benefit.

It's crucial to acknowledge these distractions but ensure they do not consume your time or resources. Learning to say no to Junk Sparks is as vital as saying yes to your Passion Pursuits. Whatever falls into this category should, if possible, be decisively abandoned. Just as pruning helps a garden thrive by removing unhealthy or overgrown branches, effectively managing your distractions by eliminating Junk Sparks can enhance your focus and productivity in areas that truly matter.

This quadrant is particularly active for many people in today's world, given the easy access to information and the constant exposure to other people's stories and achievements. It's human nature to observe what others are doing and desire it for ourselves rather than appreciating what we already have. By recognizing how frequently we are pushed and pulled in new directions, it becomes essential to understand what exactly is exerting this influence.

Then, we must consciously—and proudly—say, "Nope, that's cool, but not for me."

Honestly, this is my most filled-in quadrant as I get a lot of Junk Sparks because I get inspired by so many things. Examples include:

- starting a software project in 2010 that didn't go anywhere (I'll tell that story later);
- starting to stream games on Twitch, because I like playing video games (like Fortnite) and wanted to be a pro gamer (which did not happen);

- creating a meal prep service, because I needed help with meal prep myself and thought it would be a good idea to create recipes for others who wanted the same (the results were not favorable);
- creating a video channel for IKEA furniture to help people learn how to put them together (because those directions are impossible to understand!);
- starting a website about reviews for wireless headphones;
- becoming a logo designer just because I was good at it and helped a friend do it once;
- and many, many more.

It goes without saying that none of these led to any major breakthroughs (unless you are one of the three people who found my IKEA furniture channel—in which case, welcome!). Over time, however, I've learned to control this urge (somewhat), and we'll learn in later chapters how to do the same so we can remain focused.

Most Junk Sparks are just random ideas that need to be reined in. Otherwise, you waste a lot of time and energy chasing the latest thing that's grabbed your attention. Saying *no* is one of the most crucial skills we can develop to accelerate our learning. Every time we say *yes* to something new, we are not choosing something else. By mastering the art of refusal, we recommit to the commitments that truly deserve our time and attention. Consider asking yourself the following:

- "Is this truly adding value to my life, or is it merely appealing because it's popular or visible right now?"
- "What am I sacrificing by indulging in this distraction?"
- "Does this align with my long-term goals and values, or is it just a momentary diversion?"

By applying these filters, you not only protect your time and energy but also ensure your focus remains on enriching pursuits that align with your core interests and aspirations.

4. Critical Commitments

These tasks may not be glamorous or exciting, but they are essential. Whether it's filing taxes, attending important trainings, or managing day-to-day operations, these endeavors are necessary for your stability and success in any area of life. Approach these tasks with a sense of duty and efficiency, allowing you to fulfill your obligations while making room for passion.

Personally speaking, as of late, my critical commitments include estate planning and updating my will. It's important to me to make sure that I have my paperwork in order for what needs to be done in the event that something tragic happens to me and/or my wife. Not fun, for sure, but definitely necessary.

Now that you understand how the Inspiration Matrix works, let's put it into action. Before we can look forward, we need a clear picture of where we currently stand. This next exercise will help you audit and map out all the projects and pursuits you're currently engaged in. By creating your own Inspiration Matrix, you'll not only see where your energies are being spent but also identify any gaps or areas that may need more attention or adjustment.

Exercise:
Create Your Own Inspiration Matrix

1. **List Your Current Pursuits:** Start by listing all your current projects, tasks, hobbies, and any other activities you regularly engage in.

2. **Categorize Each Pursuit:** Refer to the Inspiration Matrix and place each activity in one of the four quadrants: Passion Pursuits, Critical Commitments,

Recreational Inspirations, or Junk Sparks. Be honest with yourself about which quadrant they belong to based on how exciting they are and how essential they are to your goals.

3. **Visual Mapping:** Draw your matrix on a large piece of paper or use a digital tool if you prefer. Place each activity in its respective quadrant. This visual representation will help you see the balance—or imbalance—in your current pursuits.

4. **Reflect on the Distribution:** Take a moment to look at your completed matrix. Are most of your activities clustered in one quadrant? Are there areas that are neglected? This reflection can help pinpoint where you might be overextending yourself or where you need to inject more energy.

With your Inspiration Matrix in hand, you now have a visual map of your current commitments and passions. But to truly determine which of these is worth pursuing further, we need to project ourselves into the future. Are you ready to explore the future implications of your current pursuits as well as new ones? Let's dive into the possibilities that await and make informed decisions about where to focus your precious time and energy.

Going 88 MPH

Vision boards, five-year plans, and strategic roadmaps—these tools are staples in the arsenal of anyone looking to shape their future. They help us sketch out our aspirations and pave pathways toward our dreams. Yet, in my experience, while these methods frame our intentions, they don't always bring us closer to the reality of future success. So, how do we bridge the gap between planning and experiencing?

The most successful way, I've found, is not just to imagine the future, but to actually "visit" it. This isn't just another visualization technique. It's a time travel mission to your future self. What makes this thought experiment unique is that we don't stop at the launching pad of success. We propel ourselves beyond, to explore what life looks like after those goals are achieved.

This exercise has been proven to work wonders inside of the SPI Community. SPI—short for "Smart Passive Income"—started as a blog in 2008 for me to journal my business learnings and share it with others, but in 2020 the brand pivoted to a community-centered approach because we've found (and the data shows) that people are more likely to succeed when working together with other like-minded peers. Although we teach every aspect of starting and running a business, from how to find your idea to how to start a podcast, YouTube channel, email list, all the way through monetization and growing a team, it's the mindset exercises that hit the hardest.

I frequently guide our members and students through this time travel thought experiment, and it always leads to numerous revelations and a deeper understanding of the consequences of decisions made today.

Sometimes, a student will realize that the business idea they have, even if it were to succeed, would not lead them to a life of happiness and fulfillment. It's quite a jarring realization when you discover that what you've been excited about all this time isn't actually the right path for you, but it's also a gift to learn that up front. I've met too many people who have climbed up a ladder only to realize it was the wrong one. It's never too late to change your path, but the sooner you understand the direction you want to go, the better.

Other times, the opposite will happen. A trip into the future reinforces a direction and provides a boost of energy, allowing a person to more easily remove those Junk Sparks that don't align with the goal.

Before we commit to any path, then, it's crucial to consider where that decision might lead. Here's how the exercise works:

1. Choose an inspiration from your Inspiration Matrix—something you're deeply curious about, regarding its potential impact on your future.

2. Imagine stepping into the DeLorean Time Machine from *Back to the Future*.

3. Set your destination for one year ahead. As you hit the gas and accelerate to 88 miles per hour, blue

energy lightning envelops you, transporting you one year into the future, and in this particular timeline, your chosen inspiration has succeeded in every conceivable way.

4. Reflect on the following questions in this future scenario:

   - What does your daily life look like now?
   - Are you closer to your goals?
   - Who are the people around you, and what activities are you engaging in together?
   - How much regret, if any, do you feel about choosing this path over others?
   - What aspects of this future excite you the most?

5. Armed with insights from the future, return to the present to reassess or repeat the exercise with another inspiration. Remember, you have an unlimited supply of "plutonium" to explore various futures as often as you need.

This approach has been transformative for many, including one of my students, Andrew Borst. Initially, Andrew was reluctant to start his own business due to concerns about losing his disability benefits. However, through this exercise, he envisioned a future where he found greater fulfillment, and achieving that became his new goal.

Today, Andrew runs ConsultaBlindGuy.com, aiding others who are visually impaired, and his success has led him to successfully surpass the financial threshold for disability benefits. Even my own children apply this framework to consider their educational paths and extracurricular activities. By envisioning our future success and the lifestyle it entails, we can make more informed decisions that align with our deepest aspirations and long-term happiness.

Some of my students, when they venture into their imagined futures, discover that the life they thought would bring them joy doesn't quite live up to their expectations. I experienced this firsthand during a high-stakes moment in my own life—a true fork in the road.

In the early 2010s, I was presented with the opportunity to become the CEO of a hosting company. On paper, the position was incredibly appealing: a substantial salary, a large office, and the chance to lead a significant team. However, when I "traveled" into that future, I saw a life that didn't align with my deepest values and goals. I imagined living in a state that wasn't appealing to me, wearing a suit every day, and having no freedom to pursue creative projects outside of my work or spend more time with my family.

This glimpse helped me realize that this path, while lucrative and prestigious, would restrict the personal and creative freedoms I cherished so much. It made the decision to turn down the offer clear, allowing me to steer away from a future that wasn't right for me.

Will this thought experiment actually guarantee these futures will happen? No, of course not. But that's not the point. It's not the point of vision boards or roadmaps, either. The point is that it helps us sift through the clutter of possibilities, and when we lean on our inspirations, each of those left on the board gets more of our time and attention. We will be more likely to steer our lives toward the futures we truly desire. Which is why we should be clear about what those are.

After exploring different possibilities and understanding the potential of our inspirations through our time travel exercise, the next step is to commit.

Commitment is the bridge between what's possible and what becomes reality. It's about setting initial steps, defining achievable goals, and deciding on the right amount of time and resources before reevaluating. It ensures that our energies are not just well spent, but also brings us closer to the life we want to lead.

Commit to Pursue

The gap between inspiration and action is vast. Data on how many people are inspired to do something versus those who actually follow through is, frankly, disheartening.

For instance, research by psychologist Richard Wiseman reveals a stark reality: 88 percent of people who set New Year's resolutions fail to achieve them, despite 52 percent feeling confident of success at the outset. This isn't just about lacking willpower. It's an issue in how we approach goals and commitments.[1]

Personally, I've seen how even a bit of structure can dramatically increase the likelihood of a person achieving a goal. In fact, our students in the SPI Community are 37 percent more likely to succeed when they apply the strategies discussed in the upcoming chapters. We've seen it firsthand.

But we're getting ahead of ourselves. Success starts long before we dive into tactics and action plans. It begins with ensuring we're headed in the right direction, committing to learn with an open mind, and dedicating genuine effort to our pursuits. So as we wrap this chapter, it's normal to feel both a mix of excitement and doubt. Questions about timing, capability, and whether this path is truly right for you might be swirling in your mind. I recognize these doubts because I've coached countless people through them and have lived them myself.

So let's look at a handful of them.

How do I really know if my inspiration is just a fleeting interest or something worth pursuing long term?

If you've gone through the previous exercises and are still asking this question, that means you really want to make sure you're not wasting your time. I understand, but here's the truth:

The number one thing wasting your time is overthinking, overlearning, and asking too many questions before you try. The only way to truly know is to commit to taking action, and then do it.

What if I commit to a path and then discover it's not right for me?

Discovering that a path isn't right for you is not a setback; it's an insight. Losing a spark for a particular pursuit doesn't signal failure—it signals a need for redirection. It's far better to pivot early than to persist in error. We'll establish regular checkpoints in your journey to reassess and adjust your course as needed. This way, you can ensure that your energy is always aligned with what truly ignites your passion.

Remember, every step taken—even those on a detour—provides valuable lessons and clarity. Each misstep or change in direction helps refine your understanding of what you truly want and need from your pursuits. Above all, commit to a specific amount of time to actively pursue and explore each inspiration. Allow yourself the space to fully engage with a new path, but also be willing to let go if the spark fades.

When you feel a spark slipping away, ask yourself the following questions:

1. *What has changed in my interest or circumstances?*
2. *What can I learn from what didn't resonate with me?*
3. *How can I apply these insights to my next endeavor?*

This reflective process is not just about recognizing when to move on; it's about learning how to better navigate your future paths. Embrace the journey of finding what truly sparks your enthusiasm and commitment. By doing so, you transform what might seem like a loss into a powerful tool for growth and self-discovery.

How much time should I realistically dedicate to a new pursuit, especially if I have other commitments?

Deciding how much time to dedicate to a new pursuit is a personal decision that hinges on both your current commitments and your aspirations. It's important to recognize that everyone has a different amount of free hours, and what matters is how you prioritize these hours, influenced by where your new interest fits within our Inspiration Matrix.

For those pursuits categorized under Passion Pursuits, you might find it worthwhile to rearrange your schedule or even temporarily sacrifice less critical activities to make room for a potential life-changer. That could mean dedicating early mornings, late evenings, or weekends to the new pursuit, especially during an initial commitment period.

The time frame is important not only to experience the joys of the new pursuit but also to endure and learn from its inherent challenges, assessing its long-term viability. The exact amount of time depends; however, I've found personally that a commitment of six months has been sufficient before reassessing and determining whether or not something is worth continuing.

When I decided to write my first book, and it became a Passion Pursuit, I knew I needed to carve out time to write it, or it would never happen. I was able to make it work by trading one hour of TV time each night before bed for one hour of writing in the morning before anyone else in my family was awake. This became my morning routine for several months, and you know what? I don't even remember what was on TV back in 2013—but in exchange for that one hour of sacrificed television time, I published a book and since then several others that have changed the lives of many. It was definitely worth the trade.

Podcasting is another example. In 2010, I gave myself six months, or about twenty episodes, to determine whether or not I would continue with podcasting. By episode ten, though, I was in love and had gotten so much positive feedback that I knew I wasn't going to stop. There were many times within the first few episodes, however, that I wanted to give up or thought it was all for nothing. But now, with over 2,000 episodes recorded across several different shows, this one pursuit changed my life in so many ways. I'm glad I stuck with it.

If a new interest falls into the Recreational Inspirations quadrant, your approach to time allocation might be more flexible. Here, the commitment should enhance your life without causing undue stress or significant sacrifices. It's about adding joy and relaxation without disrupting the essential balance of your existing responsibilities. You might choose to spend a few hours each week on this activity, fitting it into your schedule where it naturally aligns with your other obligations.

In both cases, prioritization plays a key role. It's about making conscious choices that align with your values and long-term goals. Ask yourself:

1. **"How does this pursuit fit into my life right now?"**
   It's okay to honor the areas that you've already committed to. We all have obligations and responsibilities, and it's important to acknowledge these while we try to make room for something new.

2. **"What am I willing to adjust or forgo to accom-modate this new interest?"** We each only have twenty-four hours in a day to work with, so when we say *yes* to something new, consequently we are say-ing *no* to something else. The trick is knowing when and where to trade, and when to stick with what you once already committed to.

3. **"How does this activity serve my broader objec-tives and desires?"** Everything has a cost and a purpose. If we are going to make room for some new activity in our lives, we should know why we're doing it and what it's ultimately leading to (more on that in Chapter 6).

By thoughtfully considering these questions, you can deter-mine the most appropriate level of commitment for each quad-rant. This approach ensures that you invest your time wisely, making progress in areas that truly matter while maintaining the necessary balance across all facets of your life.

Can I pursue multiple inspirations at once, or should I focus on one at a time?

It's certainly possible to juggle multiple inspirations simul-taneously, but the key is managing your resources effectively to prevent burnout. Focusing on one inspiration at a time al-lows for deeper engagement and will lead to more significant progress.

It's easy to say but harder to practice: be realistic about what you can handle. Spreading yourself too thin can dilute the quality of your efforts in both. In later chapters, I'll share strategies for those like myself who are multidisciplinary and curious about more than one thing.

What are the first steps I should take after deciding to pursue a specific inspiration?

You're anxious to get started. Perfect. The very first step you need to take is outlined in the next chapter—an essential strategy to ensure your success. Remember that a spark alone cannot start a fire; it needs a lot of reinforcement to be fanned into flame. Think of your initial actions as kindling for your spark, carefully chosen and positioned to help your flame catch and grow. When we move from passive inspiration to active curiosity, we are no longer just spectators in this adventure of learning. We are in the game now, taking action—not just learning, but *doing*—which is what the next chapter is all about.

2.

Choosing Action over Information

"Knowledge, if it does not determine action,
is dead to us."

—Plotinus

Motivation alone won't reshape your world. Only action can transform inspiration into tangible progress. As we transition from the theoretical to the practical, this chapter focuses on converting your motivation into concrete actions. The aim is not just to plan or aspire, but to act—intentionally and effectively.

In a world overflowing with information, the true challenge is not gathering more insights but deciding to take that first, crucial step. We are about to cross over the threshold between passive learning into active learning. Think of it as the difference between plotting a journey and actually stepping out the door. Without action, the most detailed maps and plans remain just possibilities.

In my own entrepreneurial story, as a perpetual planner and seasoned procrastinator, it took just a single phrase from my business coach to finally convert my potential inspiration into kinetic, actionable progress.

JFGS

"Just freaking get started."

I clicked the end of my pen and started writing that down in my notebook.

"Stop writing shit down. There's nothing more to write, come on! Just freaking do it already!"

I had never seen my business coach this upset before. In fact, this was the first time I had ever heard him swear. I guess I pushed him to the boiling point. I had started working with Jeremy after we connected in a local entrepreneurs group. His go-to outfit was classic California casual: a short-sleeved button-down shirt, cargo shorts, and flip-flops. But behind that laid-back style, he was sharp and highly experienced, with several years of business success under his belt at that point. And I was eager to follow his lead.

We had been meeting like this every other week at the same Cheesecake Factory for a few months, but this time Jeremy was pissed. I closed my notebook and locked eyes with him, because I knew he wasn't finished with me yet. "Pat," he continued, "you have a whole notebook of strategies, but . . . you still haven't launched your book yet! You're helping nobody with a notebook full of *plans*."

He was right. I had been planning to sell an eBook to my audience of architects and designers to help them pass a difficult exam called the LEED. The test was about green building practices and sustainable design, and before I was let go from my job,

I had just passed the exam myself. I had even built a website and had thousands of people visiting the resource every single day. Despite all that, I had continued to delay the launch and kept learning more. Maybe that's why I liked the Cheesecake Factory so much, because even back in 2008, their menu was as big as it is today. I always felt like the more options I had, the better.

From the dozens of blogs and podcasts I was subscribed to at the time, to the business books I purchased from Barnes & Noble because I had already read half of the material in the store, I was always in search mode.

On the surface, I was searching for some magical answer—a *"Eureka!"* moment, you could say—some piece of content that would make my new endeavor a lot easier. But in retrospect, all I was doing was searching for something to hide behind, and that something was *learning*.

At any rate, my Chicken Madeira was getting cold, and Jeremy had just lit a fire beneath me. He saw what I couldn't—that all my knowledge was actually getting in the way of doing something. It was time to get started. And if you're anything like I was, the same may be true for you.

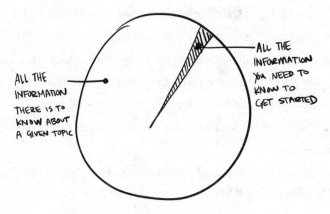

As you and I move forward in this process, you'll discover various strategies designed to propel you into taking those initial steps and maintain momentum as you go. These methods have helped me and thousands of others transform preparation into performance. Later in this book, we'll explore ways to navigate through the distractions of endless content that can steer you off course. At this point, you're probably poised to take action, as I was that day after my heart-to-heart with Jeremy. But perhaps there's still something holding you back, something you can't quite overcome—and that's not knowing what your first steps should be.

To help you pinpoint your next moves with precision, I'm going to show you the most direct route to clear and actionable steps. And it starts with a simple key question, one that changes everything.

The Keystone Question: ITWEWWILL?

This question, inspired by Tim Ferriss, is a question I ask myself when I find myself overwhelmed, paralyzed by choice or just confused and frustrated with something I'm trying to accomplish. This question has helped me in my marriage. It has helped me with my team. And it's also helping me write this book. It is the most useful and versatile question you could ever ask yourself at any moment in time when you're trying to figure out what to do next:

"If this were easy, what would it look like?" (ITWEWWILL)

It. We will.

ITWEWWILL is the Keystone Question of this entire chapter. It is the key to unlocking what your next steps should be. Some people call this the minimum viable action, or MVA—the shortest, simplest version of what it takes to get a result, and it's somewhat akin to the principle of *first principles*, popularized by visionaries like Elon Musk. But in my view, ITWEWWILL is the question that leads to those answers, and therefore the tool you can use at any moment, at any time, in any process.

For example, when my videographer Caleb Wojcik and I were inspired to invent a brand-new tripod for vloggers, this question became our guiding compass throughout the entire process. We partnered up to create a new business, but neither of us knew anything about creating physical products, manufacturing, or shipping, and it was this Keystone Question that helped us figure out what to do next.

During the prototyping phase we asked ourselves, "If this were easy, what would it look like?," and we simply cut various shapes out of cardboard boxes we already had lying around. When trying to determine what the proper dimensions of our product should be, we asked ourselves the same question, and decided to drive to a YouTuber conference (VidCon) and just ask the creators who were there.

And when deciding to sell our product, that same question helped us understand that building relationships with influential people would be way more valuable than trying to nail advertisement campaigns. With everything we learned along the way, the SwitchPod officially launched on the crowdfunding platform Kickstarter in January of 2019. A total of 4,418 backers helped us earn $415,748 in just 60 days. Today, we've sold over

$2 million in product, have partnered with major retailers in the photography and videography industries, and even had our product for sale at Best Buy.

After our public launch, we asked ourselves that all-important question once more, and found that the easiest way to expand the company was not to buy warehouses, hire more employees, and fight for more market share. We didn't have the time or resources to do all of that. Rather, we decided to add accessories to our main product, such as a ball-head attachment and a mobile phone adapter. Instead of inventing these products from scratch, we white-labeled them from manufacturing partners who had designs already made that we could adjust slightly. We then sold all of those products individually, and as a total package.

As a result of these choices, the revenue grew even more with relatively little work. This was the perfect scenario for where my partner and I were in our lives, as he and his wife had just had twins, and I was dedicating a lot more time to the new Pokémon YouTube channel I'd recently launched, while maintaining SPI and its new communities. This is the power of asking ourselves the same ITWEWWILL question multiple times across the various stages of a launch. Because at each stage, we can make decisions that affect our real-time situation versus trying to build an entire five- to ten-year business plan. Because who knows what will happen, how our lives (and our goals) will change?

ITWEWWILL also helped Kelvin Doe, a young innovator from Sierra Leone, learn about electronics and create his own inventions. Kelvin grew up in a community with limited access to education and resources, but he didn't let that stop him. He simply asked himself, "If learning about electronics were easy, what would it look like?"

For Kelvin, the answer was clear: he would learn by doing, using whatever resources he could find. So, at the age of ten, he started collecting discarded electronic parts from trash bins and dumpsites.

With curiosity and creativity as his guides, Kelvin taught himself how these devices worked by taking them apart and tinkering with them. He then applied his knowledge to real-world problems, building a battery to power homes in his community and a radio transmitter to broadcast news and music.

Kelvin's story shows that when we strip away the perceived barriers to learning and focus on what we can do with the resources at hand, we open up a world of possibilities. With a Lean Learning mindset, Kelvin transformed scrap parts into life-changing inventions, all without fancy labs or extensive resources.

The question "If this were easy, what would it look like?" serves as a powerful reminder that we don't need perfect conditions to begin learning and creating. You can start exactly where you are, with whatever you have.

Right now, as you're reading this, if you haven't yet applied this Keystone Question to your current inspiration, take a moment. Pause, reflect, and ask yourself, "If this were easy, what would it look like?"

Embracing Imperfection

As you stand ready to take your first steps toward a new venture or goal, it's natural to experience a mixture of anticipation and anxiety, and as you enter the unknown, your first instinct may be to go back to learning more. The more you know, the better off you'll be, right? We already know that's not true.

The extra learning you're turning to is getting in the way of action. It's like a weighted safety blanket that's so heavy, you're never going to move out from under it. At least it's comfortable, which is the exact state you want to be in if you don't want to grow or change. After you know what your first steps are, there's no new information that can help you. New information is likely to confuse and overwhelm you, thrusting you into a vicious cycle of worry, learning, back to worry, to learning more, and so on. The information you actually need is on the other side of those actions. Messing up is stepping up.

As John Lee Dumas, a friend and host of the popular podcast *Entrepreneurs on Fire*, once said, "You have to be a disaster before you become the master." Or, as I like to say to members in our community going through our YouTube material, "You have to be cringe before they binge." Same idea. You will be bad, you will be imperfect, and because of that, you will learn faster.

If you were conditioned like I was to believe mistakes were bad and failing should be avoided at all costs, then we're going to need to work on that. That will actually hold you back more than anything.

The Unexpected Value of Mistakes

In our society today, we tend to demonize failure. We think it's the enemy. But the truth is failure is a necessary step to success. This is at the heart of most start-up communities; it's how people who work in technology can build great things. As Mark Zuckerberg said early on in the days of Facebook: "Move fast and break things."

For the Lean Learner, mistakes are more than missteps. They are learning opportunities that offer deeper insights than most successes will ever teach. Every error invites you to examine its cause, understand its context, and learn lessons most textbooks and advice could never impart. This hands-on approach to skill acquisition deepens your understanding and equips you for future challenges.

But not all failures, of course, are created equal. Harvard researcher Amy Edmondson talks about the different kinds of mistakes we make, identifying the three main types of failures:

- basic failures—where we have access to the "right way" of doing something, but we just don't follow it;
- complex failures—where we fail due to the combination of factors that create new complexities in otherwise familiar circumstances; and
- intelligent failures—where we do not get the results we anticipate when attempting something new in a new context.

As Edmondson writes in her now famous *Harvard Business Review* article, "It's OK to Fail, but You Have to Do It Right."[1]

But, *how*? How do we fail well?

How do we do something our parents, teachers, and peers taught us was wrong?

By doing it intelligently. By taking relatively small risks in psychologically safe ways where the potential upside is high and the potential low side is pretty low. Intelligent failure is innovation recontextualized. It means tackling new ideas in new spaces and doing it in ways where you can easily recover. That way, there's always something to learn.

When we learn to fail well—when we do it intelligently—we build resilience, create more opportunities for innovation, and understand our skill at a deeper level.

Mistakes Lead to Understanding

Mistakes are invaluable opportunities for deeper comprehension. When you make a mistake, you are forced to pause and reflect, breaking down the elements of your actions to understand where things went wrong. This process naturally deepens your understanding of any activity.

One of the primary ways mistakes lead to understanding is through the immediate feedback they provide. Unlike theoretical knowledge, which can be abstract and disconnected from real-world application, mistakes offer concrete (and sometimes harsh) lessons about what does not work. This feedback is crucial as it directs your next steps more accurately than success can.

When you succeed, it's often unclear which specific actions contributed to the outcome. Mistakes, by contrast, clearly highlight deficiencies and misconceptions, urging you to investigate and adapt.

Making mistakes also naturally stimulates curiosity. You might ask, "Why did this happen?" or "What can I do differently next time?" This type of questioning is fundamental to learning and leads to a deeper dive into the mechanics of your activities. It encourages you to go beyond surface-level understanding and explore the underlying principles at work, which is essential for true mastery.

Furthermore, the emotional response to making a mistake—whether frustration, disappointment, or discouragement—is a powerful teacher. Learning to manage these emotions and transform them into productive energy is a vital aspect of personal and professional development. This emotional management is a form of understanding that transcends the specific task and becomes a lifelong skill.

Understanding through mistakes is rarely a one-off event. It involves a cycle of trying, failing, learning, and trying again. This iterative process is at the heart of agile methodologies—which are designed to help creators and developers thrive within complex conditions where change is the norm—and lean start-up principles—where you've got to move quickly and recover even faster so that you don't get left behind.

In these cases, whether it's in a business context or you're building a web app, rapid iterations based on continuous feedback loops are preferred over extensive planning and perfect execution. This ensures that learning is continuous and improvements are made incrementally, which will lead to better long-term outcomes. Incorporating these insights into your learning journey can transform the way you perceive and react to mistakes, turning them from sources of embarrassment into powerful catalysts for growth.

Mistakes Lead to Resilience

Building resilience through mistakes is a crucial skill for anyone aiming to succeed in challenging environments. When you encounter setbacks and learn to overcome them, you not only gain specific knowledge about the task but also develop mental and emotional toughness. This resilience is what prepares you to face and conquer future challenges.

In October of 2008, when I launched my first business to help architects pass the LEED exam, it wasn't originally called *Green Exam Academy*, which is the name today. The original name was *In the LEED*, which I thought was a clever and memorable pun for anyone studying for the exam.

When I looked at my books on December 31 of the same year, I saw that I had already generated more revenue in those short three months than what was my annual salary when I still had my job. Things were rolling, and each month my revenue continued to climb.

In May of 2009, I received a letter in the mail from the U.S. Green Building Council (USGBC). I had originally thought it was to thank me for my work for helping people earn their credential, or maybe a request to partner on exam material, but I was wrong. Very wrong. It was a cease-and-desist letter, and in it, they said I had only fourteen days to take my business down, or else there would be further legal action.

I had made the big rookie mistake of using a trademark in my brand and domain name. LEED was a mark owned by the USGBC, and I was using it at IntheLEED.com without permission. And in order to protect their brand and avoid consumer confusion, they went after me and my business. Mentally, I shut down. I was done. I took this as a giant sign that I was not cut out for running my own business, and I remember telling myself, "This is what happens when you don't go to business school."

Looking back, I scoff at that remark. To think that going to business school—dedicating tens of thousands of dollars plus several more years of education—would somehow have saved me is a wild thought. Sure, perhaps I'd be smarter with my approach when choosing a name, but I also know they weren't teaching anything about how to build a website, increase search engine rankings on Google, or write and sell your own eBooks on a website—which I was learning to do in real time. Instead, I could have done a little bit of research when I was selecting my brand name and avoided the situation.

Unfortunately, I didn't do that and had just fourteen days to figure things out.

This experience became my real-time business school in regard to trademark and legal matters for businesses like mine. The day after the letter came, I hired an attorney to help walk me through my options, and within ten days I was able to change the brand name to *Green Exam Academy*, and I also figured out how to keep my search engine rankings.

After the dust settled, the USGBC reached out to me and actually said they enjoyed my website and were thankful for the work I was doing. They also apologized for the stern approach their lawyers took in that initial letter. Other than wishing we had this cordial conversation first, I was grateful for the experience overall.

Imagine if I had quit because of what had happened? I was so close to running away and giving up entirely, that I actually did check to see if there were any local job openings for architects. Thankfully, no one called back.

This ordeal taught me invaluable lessons about resilience and the importance of adaptability in business. Facing the potential collapse of my first entrepreneurial venture, I learned that resilience isn't just about bouncing back from setbacks; it's about using those setbacks as stepping-stones to evolve and strengthen your approach.

Now, whenever I face challenges, instead of shutting down, I actively seek solutions and explore alternatives, much like how I navigated the trademark issue. This proactive attitude has not only helped me in maintaining my businesses but has also instilled a mindset where I view every challenge as an opportunity to learn and improve. I now transform potential defeats into drivers of growth and innovation.

To give a less personal example, think of the restaurants that struggled during the Covid pandemic. Some went under while others reimagined how they could deliver food to patrons and embraced online deliveries. As a result, those that became more resilient thrived. I'm sure this wasn't an easy move to make for many restaurants, but it became necessary. Sometimes, it's not a mistake that causes us to grow but simply a change in circumstances. How we adapt, though, determines whether or not we thrive.

Mistakes Lead to Innovation

Many of the world's greatest innovations have stemmed from happy accidents. These mistakes often open doors to new ways of thinking and unexpected pathways to success. By embracing mistakes, you allow yourself the freedom to explore and the potential to discover something truly groundbreaking.

The discovery of penicillin by Alexander Fleming is a classic example of innovation born from a mistake. Fleming's accidental contamination of a petri dish led to the realization that mold could kill bacteria, revolutionizing medical treatment and saving millions of lives. Similarly, tech companies like Instagram and Slack pivoted from their original business models only after recognizing that their initial plans were failing to catch on, leading to the successful platforms we know today.

YouTube is another example. It launched on Valentine's Day in 2005 as a dating website where one could upload a video about themselves in hopes of finding a partner. When no one was uploading videos for that purpose, the platform allowed anyone to publish videos about anything, and thus the first YouTube video filmed in my hometown of San Diego, California, titled *Me at the Zoo*, was published. And the rest is history.

The Truth About Fear

If I were to go back in time and teach something to my younger self to set myself up for success, I would tell myself two things. First, that JNCO jeans are not as cool as you think. And second, I'd have an honest conversation with young Pat about fear.

Fear kept me from embracing many opportunities and potential life experiences—not only during my teenage years and college days but also deep into my career as an architect. There's a 99.99 percent chance that if I hadn't been laid off in 2008, I would never have ventured into business and entrepreneurship. It wasn't a lack of curiosity that held me back, but rather the fear of failure and concern over what others might think that outweighed the opportunities before me.

Fear manifests in various subtle forms and masquerades as rational excuses or delays in action. Recognizing these symptoms is the first step in overcoming them.

Symptoms of Fear

Procrastination is one of the most common symptoms of fear. It's not just laziness or poor time management; it's a deep-seated fear of failure or judgment that keeps us from starting or completing tasks. Other symptoms include overplanning, where we get stuck in the details instead of moving forward, and perpetual learning, where we continuously seek out more information instead of applying what we know.

We also tell ourselves that "now's not the right time," or we wait for the perfect moment when we feel fully prepared—

which, of course, never arrives. These excuses are fear's way of keeping us in our comfort zone, safe from potential failure or criticism.

Addressing Fear Head-on

To combat these fears, we must first acknowledge them. As Steven Pressfield points out in *The War of Art*, resistance is most powerful at the finish line. The closer we get to achieving our goals, the more intense our fears become. Recognizing this pattern can help us push through the resistance we feel in any endeavor.

1. **Acknowledge the fear:** First and foremost, we have to admit when our anxiety and self-doubt are holding us back. When we do this, it's like looking in the closet you're scared to peek into as a kid, seeing if there's really a monster in there. When we acknowledge our fears, we diminish their power.

2. **Challenge procrastination:** When you notice yourself procrastinating, ask yourself what, exactly, you're afraid of. Only then can you begin to work through it and overcome it. Then, you challenge your fear by setting small but manageable goals that help you build momentum and grow in confidence.

3. **Overcome overplanning:** Simplify your plans. Break down your goals into actionable steps that

focus more on doing and less on planning. Remember, no plan survives contact with reality, and flexibility is key.

4. **Redefine readiness:** Redefine what it means to be ready. Embrace the idea that starting before you feel ready can actually be an advantage, as it forces you to adapt and learn quickly.

5. **Embrace imperfection:** Allow yourself to be imperfect and acknowledge that mistakes are not failures but opportunities to learn and improve. This mindset will reduce the fear of judgment and failure.

6. **Use fear as a catalyst:** Instead of allowing fear to paralyze us, we can use it as a catalyst for growth. When we feel fear, it's a signal that we're pushing beyond the familiar and our current limits and entering into new, potentially rewarding territories. By reframing fear as a positive sign of growth and learning, we can transform our approach to challenges and uncertainty. As I've learned, the fear doesn't actually go away. I still fear the outcome of new projects and opportunities. However, I've learned to understand what that fear means, and how to convert that into something positive, a signal that I'm headed in the right direction. In fact, it is the absence of fear that concerns me more, as it may suggest a lack of challenge or innovation or enthusiasm in what I'm pursuing.

Trading Your "What If's" for "Oh Well's"

To cap off our exploration of taking action over gathering information, let's jump into our DeLorean and travel back to the future (see what I did there?)—not just a year this time, but ten years ahead. As you look at the coming decade, imagine the impact of the decisions you're hesitating to make today. What will you wish you had started *now*? What ideas might you regret not pursuing? Ten years from now, will you look back with gratitude for the courageous choices you made today, regardless of whether they worked out as planned?

This is not just about avoiding negative outcomes but about embracing opportunities that align with your deepest aspirations. The regret of inaction can actually be more profound than the regret of failure. Trust me, I've felt them both. The unlived life is always more painful than a few embarrassing mistakes that only take some time and maybe a few apologies to recover from. Unlike the mistakes from which we learn and grow, the opportunities we never seize leave us with a lingering series of "what if" scenarios.

What *if* we had been braver?

What *if* we had actually gone after that dream?

What *if* we risked more?

By taking this broader view of what's to come, you can see how today's decisions shape your future. This perspective turns our fear of starting into a motivation to proceed, transforming potential regret into a powerful catalyst for action.

Look, you won't do any of this perfectly—that's a given—but let's ensure when you look back on the next ten years that your timeline is filled with bold attempts and growth, not just the echoes of hesitation. Your future self doesn't want to live with that regret, I guarantee it.

This approach is more than an exercise. It's a lifestyle shift that helps us live more proactively and minimize our potential future regrets. Personally, I'd rather live a life full of "oh well's" than a life filled with "what if's." But that's just me. What you do is, of course, up to you.

Understanding our fears and embracing imperfection is not about settling for mediocrity. It's about understanding that the road to achievement is paved with unexpected twists and turns. Each step forward, each misstep, each correction is integral to your growth. This journey is as much about building resilience and adaptability as it is about achieving your goals.

But, of course, where we are and who we're with determine how successful we can be. When it comes to learning, environment is everything. It's not enough to simply choose action. You have to reinforce what you do with the kind of people who can guide and support you. Even geniuses need collaborators.

Doc Brown was nothing without Marty, after all. And you and I need our champions, as well.

3.

The Power of Champions:
Harnessing Mentorship
and Community

"Alone, we can do so little; together, we can do so much."

—Helen Keller

Nobody achieves greatness alone. Usually, it's the champions in our lives—those who believe in us and push us beyond our perceived limits—who help us navigate the challenges we face. As we move from the internal work of reshaping what it means to make mistakes and overcome our own fears to the external support that amplifies our potential, we meet individuals who exemplify the power of having champions in our corner.

One such champion is Dr. Barbara Cohen, affectionately known as "Dr B."

Dr B had a smile that lit up the room when I first met her in 2017 at a business and marketing conference in Anaheim, California. But beneath her warm exterior, I could sense a hint of nervousness. At the age of sixty-five, she was about to embark on a journey that she never would have imagined herself undertaking—launching her own podcast.

As a seasoned coach and mentor, Dr B had spent years helping individuals, couples, and families navigate the challenges of ADHD. Her passion for making a difference in people's lives was palpable, but she had never considered podcasting as a means to reaching a wider audience. In fact, she rarely listened to podcasts herself and didn't only consider herself challenged by technology—she was deathly afraid of it.

Yet, something had shifted in her at that conference. A spark had been ignited by a story she'd heard about the power of podcasting to touch lives and make a difference. Dr B had always dreamed of positively influencing a million people in her lifetime, and at that moment, she realized podcasting could be the vehicle to scale her impact.

But as she stood on the precipice of this new adventure, Dr B knew she couldn't do this alone. She needed guidance, support, and a community of like-minded individuals who could help her navigate the technical and emotional challenges of launching a podcast. Unfortunately, communities of up-and-coming podcasters didn't exist back then, which is what brought us together.

At this marketing conference, I was invited to speak to a room of about 1,000 people about podcasting. At the time, my own show, *The Smart Passive Income Podcast*, had just crossed 25 million downloads and was the #4 ranked business podcast in the U.S. Beyond that, it was the number-one way new people were discovering my brand, so of course the interest on how this all worked was high.

After my presentation, I invited anyone to join me in an experimental community of aspiring podcasters who wanted to learn how to launch their show. This wasn't just a do-it-yourself program, however. Those already existed on the market. What I was offering, in addition to the education, was a connection to other students, as well as access to myself as their guide.

Dr B and 134 other aspiring podcasters were on board, and almost immediately everyone began to feel a sense of camaraderie and encouragement. They were all in this together, learning from each other's successes and struggles. With each passing day, Dr B's nervousness began to fade, replaced by a growing excitement and determination to make her vision a reality.

By April 2017, she officially launched her show, *Living Beyond ADHD*, which she produced for over six years before refocusing efforts elsewhere to support the ADHD community. To this day, Dr B continues to offer resources to people struggling with ADHD and a lack of focus. When I interviewed her about her experience and asked her how she was able to overcome her challenges, it was clear it wasn't just information that helped. Dr B told me it was "because of the community." That's how any of us make big gains—we can't do it alone.

Dr B's journey to becoming a podcaster is a testament to the transformative power of community and mentorship. While scared of technology and without traditional learning, she immersed herself in this new world of podcasting and found that the support and encouragement of her fellow learners were invaluable. In her own words: "The support that we have in the group, from other members, that support made it possible to move ahead. There wasn't any point where I got completely stalled out and derailed, and I think that's very, very important."

This sense of community not only helped Dr B overcome technical challenges but also provided a safe space for her to take risks and step outside her comfort zone. She knew that even if she stumbled, there would be people there to help her get back on her feet. A community, she told me, "isn't about one person going ahead and being successful. It's about everyone . . . No one is left behind. We move together."

Her experience highlights a crucial truth about Lean Learning: no matter what you're trying to achieve, having the right people in your corner can make all the difference. These champions come in many forms and play different roles in your growth and success. However, it's not just the type of champion that matters, but also how they support you.

Whether it's emotional support, professional guidance, or personal challenges, the way your champions show up can be just as important as the role they play. But the concept of championing isn't just about receiving support; it's also about giving it. The strength of a community comes from its reciprocity— everyone contributes, everyone benefits.

As Dr B's story so beautifully demonstrates, being part of a supportive community not only means you have others to lean on but also that you have the opportunity to support others in return. This mutual exchange enriches the learning experience and amplifies the impact of the community. Each member, by supporting others, learns not only about their own capabilities but also about the power of empathy and encouragement.

Frankly, our society has strayed too far from these communal interactions, which historically formed the bedrock of learning and development. We've isolated ourselves, glorifying solo achievements while neglecting the profound benefits of collective growth. It's time we return to our roots, reembracing the communal ethos that empowers everyone to not just succeed alone, but thrive together.

So, as you navigate your own challenges and successes, consider how you can also be a champion for others. Whether it's offering a word of encouragement, sharing a valuable resource, or simply listening to someone's concerns, your actions can help propel someone else forward. This reciprocal relationship doesn't just strengthen others; it also deepens your own understanding and enhances your journey.

In this way, Lean Learning becomes a shared endeavor—not just about personal achievement but about lifting others as we climb. As Dr B said, "No one is left behind. We move together." By embedding this principle of reciprocity early in your journey, you plant the seeds for a richer, more supportive learning environment that grows with you.

I didn't always believe in the power of community though. In fact, I held myself back because I was too prideful to think I needed others around me. As you'll see, it was a huge mistake.

Letting Go to Grow

When I first started my online business, I wanted to do everything on my own. Even if another person was kind enough to offer assistance, I refused. In times of desperate need, my default response was to learn more so that I could figure out how to solve the problem on my own. My motto was *learn harder*, which is ironic, because I learned a hard lesson in the end.

In early 2008, when I was first setting up my LEED exam website, there was an image on the right side of my homepage that I wanted to move to the top, but I couldn't figure out how to do it. Blog after blog, tutorial after tutorial, I found myself on the corners of the internet turning over every virtual stone I could find, growing more frustrated with each moment. For three straight days, eight hours per day, I tried to figure it out on my own. Finally, after nonstop research and trial and error, my very patient fiancée (now wife), April, stepped in. She could tell I was super frustrated and decided to do something about it.

Without warning, April handed me her phone. Surprised, I grabbed it. "Hello?" I said, still in a daze from the three days of research I'd done. On the other end was Mel, a friend of April's from college who had recently gotten a job as a website developer. In less than five minutes, Mel solved my problem, and when I asked if there was anything he wanted in return, he said, "I just want to hang with you guys." In an instant, my frustrations with the website were gone, and my only wish was that I had asked for help sooner.

Growing up, I had been conditioned to believe that asking for help was a sign of weakness, and I didn't want to burden others with my challenges. But as I struggled to navigate the complexities of entrepreneurship, I realized this self-reliant mindset was limiting my potential. As I began to open up and share my journey with others, I discovered the power of mutual support. My champions were eager to offer their guidance and encouragement, not because they felt obligated but because they believed in me and wanted to contribute to my success.

In turn, I found ways to support them in their endeavors, creating a cycle of reciprocity that deepened our relationship and fueled our collective growth. We all can do this. By embracing vulnerability and reaching out to others, we not only accelerate our own growth but create opportunities for meaningful collaboration and mutual support with others. I've personally had many life-changing experiences as a result of connecting with various levels of champions.

For example, my wife was there when I got laid off. She struggled with me through many tough moments in business, like when I got that cease-and-desist letter from the exam council or after any number of failed product launches (and there were many!). She was always there, no matter the situation, to help me dust myself off and figure out what was the next step—a true champion for me.

Champions are a vital component in the Lean Learning model, and in this chapter we'll explore how you can cultivate these relationships, leverage their support to achieve big goals, and give back to others in equal measure.

As Dr B discovered, when you surround yourself with the right people, even the most daunting challenges become achievable. Because the truth is: your problems are not just yours. When you reach out to other people, you realize you're not so alone. Others have faced much of the same situations that you've struggled with and come out on the other side. When we look to the power of community to help us tackle whatever challenges are in our way, we are not just gaining new skills and knowledge but also the confidence and resilience to keep pushing toward our dreams.

(For the resources mentioned in this chapter, such as where you can find Dr B and her work in the world of ADHD, as well as the podcasting and business community she took part in, visit LeanLearningBook.com.)

Different Types of Champions

For many people, finding champions in their lives is something that happens naturally, without conscious effort. Friends, family members, colleagues, and mentors emerge over time, providing support and guidance as we navigate our personal and professional journeys.

However, if you want to take your learning and growth to the next level, actively building your team of champions can make all the difference.

By intentionally seeking out and cultivating relationships with individuals who can support, challenge, and inspire you, you give yourself the best possible chance of achieving your goals and realizing your full potential.

As you read through the following sections on each type of champion, take a moment to reflect on the people in your own life who may already be playing these roles, and consider how you can deepen and enhance those connections. And how you may be a champion in someone else's life.

Friends and Family

Our friends and family members tend to be our earliest and most enduring champions. These are the people who have known us the longest, who have seen us at our best and worst, and who have a deep, personal investment in our happiness and success. When it comes to building your team of champions, don't overlook the power of these intimate connections.

Start by openly sharing your goals, dreams, and challenges with them. Let them know how much you value their support and encouragement, and be specific about the ways in which they can help you. This might involve asking for emotional support during tough times, seeking advice on a particular problem, or simply having someone to celebrate your victories with.

At the same time, be sure to reciprocate by being a champion for your friends and family members in return. Take an active interest in their lives, offer your own insights and encouragement, and be there for them when they need you. By cultivating a culture of mutual support and empowerment, you create a powerful foundation of love and trust that can sustain you through even the most challenging times.

For me, my wife and my kids offer this kind of championing support more than anything. They may not know exactly what I'm needing help with or be able to offer any specific advice related to certain business goals that I have, but when I'm frustrated I know they'll listen, and when we celebrate, we celebrate together.

It's important to acknowledge that not everyone has immediate access to supportive friends and family members. In some cases, the people closest to us may not understand or approve of our goals and aspirations, which can be incredibly challenging and isolating. As someone who has personally dealt with this situation, I know firsthand how painful it can be to feel like you're going against the grain or disappointing those you love. It's okay to protect this part of you.

In these moments, it's crucial to remember that you are not alone and that there are other sources of support available to you. Remember, your worth and potential are not defined by the opinions of others, even those closest to you. By surrounding yourself with champions who believe in you and support your vision, you create a powerful foundation for growth and success.

And who knows—as you begin to thrive and achieve your goals, you may even find that your friends and family come around in time. But even if they don't, know that you have the power to build the support system you need to achieve your dreams, which takes us into our next category of champions.

———

Peers

Peer champions are the people who are walking a similar path to your own, facing the same challenges, and working toward comparable goals and inspirations. These are your colleagues, classmates, and fellow learners, the individuals who understand the ins and outs of your industry or field and who can offer a unique form of support and collaboration.

Back in high school and college, it wasn't uncommon to see peer study groups scattered around the library and bookstores, cramming for midterms or final exams. Now imagine that same format, but while taking action.

To find peer champions while you progress, seek out communities aligned with your interests and aspirations. This may involve joining professional associations, attending conferences and workshops, or actively engaging in online forums and social media groups. A prime example of the power of structured communal engagement is a CrossFit gym, where members foster mutual growth and accountability. From that connective tissue, a shared and common language is formed. If you know what a WOD is, then you're probably a CrossFitter yourself—or perhaps close to one that always talks about the Workout of the Day.

My favorite form of peer support comes from smaller, tight-knit groups of four to five people. Known as mastermind groups in the business world, these consistent gatherings provide a space for members to openly share challenges, discuss effective strategies, and receive honest, constructive feedback consistently over time. It's like a group of advisors but more akin to a "Knights of the Round Table" situation, where no one is at the head of the table. We're all in it to help each other.

I've been involved in two such groups for over a decade each, meeting weekly via virtual conference calls. The members of each of these groups have all played a significant role in my personal and professional growth, helping me overcome mental obstacles and providing valuable business advice along the way. They help me see things I cannot because I'm too close to my work, and they share their own experiences on the common path. And as much as they've helped me, I've been there for them just the same.

Each group meets weekly and has done so for ten years— that's over 500 meetings per group, and we've gotten to know each other so well across a variety of topics (not just business, but life, relationships, and more!). I hold each of these people in high regard. They encourage me but are also brutally honest when I need it and can be a shoulder to cry on, as well.

The first group is made up of: Jaime Masters (the organized one), Shawn Stevenson (the ambitious one), Rosemarie Groner (the encouraging one), and Todd Tressider (the coach who asks tough questions). In the second group, there are: Mark Mason (the jokester who sees the positive in every situation), Michael Stelzner (the big-idea guy who envisions solutions the rest can't), Leslie Samuel (the inquisitive one who helps us think more deeply), Ray Edwards (the writer who always has the right words), and Cliff Ravenscraft (the enthusiastic one whose passion shows up in every move he makes).

Both of these groups feel like family to me. The individuals in each have helped me with things from choosing the title of my books to helping me talk through life-altering decisions related to my life, and more. These groups have helped me find peers who share a common language and understanding of the challenges we all face in business and in life, offering professional support and personal encouragement along the way.

When engaging with peers, it's important to openly share your knowledge and experiences, and be generous with your time and resources. Remember, in most peer groups, you get back what you put in. But also don't hesitate to ask for help or feedback when needed, and remain open to constructive criticism and fresh perspectives.

In my business at SPI, we shifted our primary focus in 2021 from producing online courses to solely community-powered education. By connecting our audience together in a community who can be there to support each other, we find that more people are getting the results they signed up for, and now there're more people to celebrate wins together, too.

By now, you've heard quite a bit about SPI here in this book. What started out as a blog in 2008 has since become the epicenter for forward-thinking business education and growth online—all powered by community. In addition to powerful communities like ours that change lives every day, I also strongly recommend finding individuals who have once traveled on the same path that you're on today. Mentors are like compasses for us as we trek through uncharted territories, and not all mentors are the same.

Virtual Mentors

In today's digital age, we have unprecedented access to experts and thought leaders from around the world. These virtual mentors, who share their knowledge and insights through books, courses, podcasts, and videos, can be an invaluable source of guidance and inspiration as you work toward your goals.

To find virtual mentors, start by identifying the key skills, knowledge areas, and philosophies that are most relevant to your learning journey. Then, seek out content creators who specialize in those domains and whose teaching style resonates with you.

While virtual mentors may not offer the same level of personalized guidance as a one-on-one coach or mentor, they can still play a crucial role in your growth and development. By exposing you to new ideas, challenging your assumptions, and providing a model of success to aspire to, virtual mentors can help you expand your horizons and push past your limitations.

For myself, I've had several virtual mentors over the years. As I evolved, so did my choice in who to follow and learn from. In the beginning, it was Sterling and Jay from *Internet Business Mastery*, a podcast I listened to every day.

Then it was Tim Ferriss, when learning about outsourcing.

For a while, it was Gary Vaynerchuk, who taught me how to engage with an audience on social media, and how to stay positive despite being a fan of a disappointing sports team.

After having kids, my virtual mentor became Michael Hyatt, because I saw how he grew his business while remaining deeply involved in raising his family, something I wanted for myself, too.

To get the most out of your relationships with virtual mentors, be an active and engaged learner. Participate in their online communities, ask questions, and share your own experiences and insights. Many virtual mentors are highly responsive to their audiences and may even offer opportunities for more direct interaction, such as Q&A sessions, coaching calls, or live events.

With that said, in my opinion, there is no better way to speed up the learning process and achieve your goals fast than with a specific person dedicated to supporting your goals.

Personal Mentors

Personal mentors are the individuals who work with you one-on-one, providing tailored guidance, feedback, and support as you navigate your unique challenges and opportunities. These are the coaches, advisors, and teachers who take a deep, personal interest in your growth and success, and who are willing to invest significant time and energy into helping you reach your full potential.

To find a personal mentor, start by reflecting on the specific areas of your life or work where you feel you need the most support and guidance. Then, look for individuals who have achieved success in those areas and who embody the values and qualities you aspire to.

This might involve reaching out to people in your existing network, attending events or workshops led by potential mentors, or even cold-contacting individuals whose work you admire.

When approaching a potential mentor, be clear and specific about what you're looking for and what you're willing to bring to the relationship. Many successful people are happy to share their knowledge and experience with others, but they also want to ensure that the mentorship relationship is a good fit for both parties.

Be prepared to articulate your goals, your commitment to learning and growth, and the ways in which you believe the mentor's guidance could help you achieve your objectives.

I've worked with one-on-one mentors many times over the years, not just for business, but for all aspects of life where I wanted to learn more quickly and maximize my potential.

From a personal trainer to coach me through my first triathlon to hiring a fourteen-year-old kid to teach me how to play Fortnite so I could keep up with my son. You can learn much from someone who has once previously gone down the road you're on today, cutting through the noise, avoiding the common mistakes, and coaching you through tough situations. Not to mention, the accountability of just knowing you have to show up.

As you build your own team of champions, remember that the relationships you cultivate have the power to impact not only your own learning and growth but also the lives of those around you. By being a champion for others and sharing your own stories of transformation, you contribute to a ripple effect of positive change that extends far beyond your immediate circle.

Now that you know how valuable these types of relationships are, it's time to go and find your champions. In most cases, when I mentor my own students to audit their network and relationships, they're surprised to find that many of these people already exist in their lives. I imagine that the case could be the same for you, too. Let's find out.

Finding Your Champions

Now that you have a better understanding of the different types of champions and how they can support your learning journey, it's time to put this knowledge into action. Here are a few steps you can take right now to start building your team of champions:

1. Make a list of potential champions in each category: friends and family, peers, virtual mentors, and personal mentors. Consider who in your existing net-

work might fit these roles, and brainstorm new connections you could make.

2. Reach out to at least one person on your list in each category. Share your goals and aspirations, and express your desire for their support and guidance. Be specific about how you believe they could help you, and be open to their feedback and suggestions.

3. Join or create a peer group related to your interests or goals. This could be an online community, a local meetup group, or even a small mastermind group of your own creation. Commit to actively participating and contributing to the group, and look for opportunities to collaborate and support one another.

4. Identify one virtual mentor whose work resonates with you, and commit to diving deep into their content. Set aside dedicated time to consume their materials, take notes, and implement their strategies in your own life and work. While it's important to immerse yourself in learning, be mindful not to fall into the trap of overconsumption. Balance is key; absorb enough to inspire and inform your actions without becoming so engrossed that it hinders your progress. If possible, engage with their online community and look for opportunities to connect with them directly. This approach ensures that you are not just passively consuming information but actively using it to drive real change in your life.

5. Reflect on your current learning and growth challenges, and consider whether working with a per-

sonal mentor could help you overcome them. If so, start researching potential mentors and reach out to them with a clear, compelling request for guidance.

Remember, building your team of champions is an ongoing process. As you grow and evolve, so too will your relationships and support systems. Stay open to new connections, be generous with your own knowledge and resources, and always be willing to both give and receive support.

By cultivating a strong team of champions, you'll be well equipped to tackle any learning challenge that comes your way. But remember, your champions can only take you so far. As we conclude this chapter, and you continue to advance, be aware that new challenges will inevitably arise—not just from within, but from the world around you.

External influences, distractions, and unforeseen obstacles can derail even the most well-planned projects. Therefore, it's crucial not just to act, but also to protect the progress you've made. As we transition into the next chapter, we will focus on strategies to shield your journey from these external forces, ensuring that your path toward your goals remains clear and uninterrupted.

4.

Protect Your Progress

"Success is not final, failure is not fatal:
it is the courage to continue that counts."

—Winston Churchill

As much as the world is full of opportunities, it's also crammed with distractions and obstacles that can knock us off our path. We're all familiar with the usual suspects—like the endless scroll on social media or the constant dings from our phones that shatter our focus. But sometimes, the real trouble comes from things we think are helping us, but actually do the opposite. These can be the sneakiest distractions because they look like they're on our side, when really they're just slowing us down.

To keep pushing forward and maintain our momentum and focus, it's crucial to spot these hidden traps. Imagine creating a custom filter—a kind of mental armor—that lets in only the good stuff and keeps out the bad. This way, we stay on track, filtering out the noise and focusing on what truly moves us toward our goals. If only my buddy Terry knew how to do the same. Let me tell you about Terry.

Back when I was employed at my architectural firm, there

was one day of the week I looked forward to more than any other: Sunday.

Why? Because like clockwork, at exactly 6:30 a.m., I would tee off at Hole #1 at the Corica Park Golf Course in Alameda, California, with my two closest work buddies, Terry and George. This wasn't just a game to us, however. It was our weekly ritual, a sacred few hours where we left behind blueprints and building codes for irons and greens. Plus, it always made for a fun Monday back at the office.

We all wanted to be great at golf, but Terry took it to a whole new level. He was not just interested in the sport—he was obsessed with it. At work, it wasn't uncommon to catch him watching the latest golf news on his computer which sat next to his growing stack of *Golf Magazine*. His clubs were always in the trunk of his car, except for the putter, which was at his desk so that during breaks he could practice putting with one of those automatic golf ball return machines. On the course, his golf bag was always meticulously organized and each of his clubs had a head cover sporting his alma mater, Stanford. As a Cal grad, I didn't hold that against him—*too* much.

Based on this, you'd expect Terry to be great at golf, right? I did, too, until the first time we played together and he continually shanked the ball out of bounds, and over a couple of years, I didn't notice that much improvement. Only more frustration. After every mishit, you could hear Terry coaching himself under his breath and then taking a few practice swings to correct himself. It didn't seem to work.

George, on the other hand, wasn't as obsessed with golf as Terry was, at least not on the outside. George was my project manager and there was nothing in his office other than a signed golf ball that would indicate he played the game. Monday to Friday, it was all business. Then on Sundays, after playing eighteen holes together, the results were always the same—George annihilated us both.

George is what's known as a "scratch golfer," someone who doesn't need the extra bonus points or handicap required for less talented golfers (like Terry and me) to compete with those who are better. He was never a professional golfer, and he wasn't one of those gifted players with natural-born talent. He learned from scratch like the rest of us, but it became apparent that the way he approached golf—and likely other parts of his life, too—helped him get better results, faster.

George was the best boss I ever had. He taught me most of what I learned as an architect and coached me on my way to becoming the youngest Job Captain in the firm's history. And when it came to golf, you can probably guess which one of my coworkers I chose to emulate and learn from.

George's approach to golf, which starkly contrasted with Terry's, offers a valuable lesson in efficiency and focus. While Terry cluttered his mind with endless tips and theories, George, on the other hand, took a more minimalist approach. He didn't drown himself in the latest golf theories or obsess over every new piece of equipment. His focus was on playing the game and learning through doing rather than through consuming. This not only kept his mind clear of clutter but allowed him to excel at golf by keeping his technique simple and his focus sharp.

George's strategy on the golf course can teach us a lot about handling distractions in our own lives. Just as he chose to "unsubscribe" from the noise of constant golf updates and focus solely on his game, we can apply the same principle to our broader goals.

Unsubscribe from . . . *Everything*

When I first witnessed just how great George was at golf, I had to ask him, "How did you get so good?" His answer was likely disguised as a small jab at Terry: "I don't try to learn more about golf."

George didn't subscribe to any magazines, nor did he pay the extra fee to get access to the golf channel on cable. He didn't read any blogs or care about any of the news around new driver technology. He simply unsubscribed from all of it.

After a certain point in every learning journey, you know what you need to know, and all you need to do is do. Back then, this was much easier to practice. Today, it's one of the most difficult things to do.

Not only are we constantly online, but the platforms we are on are continually optimizing to give you more information that their algorithms believe you need and want. It's an arms race for attention and ad dollars, and unfortunately, we are the casualties of it.

The only way to combat this is to take decisive action, and unsubscribe and unfollow everything that does not consistently add value to your learning progress. For some, it may even require declaring "information bankruptcy," removing all sources of input, and then reengaging only with that which supports your next goal. Ideally, you'd end up with just one, maybe two at most, reliable and actionable resources that closely align with where you want to go.

Structured guidance is better than random cherry-picking. Resources like a well-designed course or a series of carefully curated content are great because they allow you to progress logically through learning materials. Combine that with guidance from someone who has already traveled the path you're on, and you can put your progress into overdrive, much like George did on the golf course.

The big question, however, is how do you know exactly what to learn, and when? This brings us to one of the most valuable lessons I've ever picked up, and it fits perfectly into our Lean Learning methodology. And right now is the right time for you to learn it.

Just-in-Time Information

I first learned about the concept of "Just-in-Time Information" (JITI) from my business coach, Jeremy. Reflecting on this, I also realized that George applied this "approach" in his golf game. Pun intended.

It's essential to start with just the information you need, but even more crucial to continue learning only what is necessary at each step. This is the essence of JITI—focusing precisely on the information required at the moment and intentionally blocking out everything else. This strategy was transformative for me, especially as a perpetual information hoarder who used to gather and store every bit of info "just in case I needed it later."

Just-in-Time Information is a crucial component of the Lean Learning process. It's all about acquiring only the information necessary to accomplish your next step, which helps prevent information overload and keeps you focused on what's most important at any given moment. Protect that next step.

Here's a quick recap of the Lean Learning process from a high level:

1. Identify the next step in your journey.
2. Gather the minimum amount of information required to complete that step.
3. Take action and complete the step.
4. Rinse and repeat.

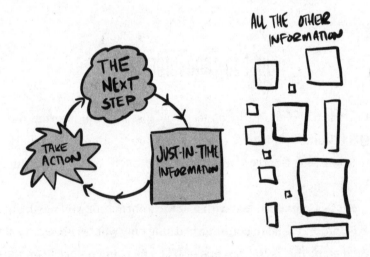

As an architect accustomed to extensively researching every detail before starting a project, this approach felt foreign and challenging. However, I wasn't designing a complex building—I was starting a business, and I needed to make progress quickly. I trusted Jeremy's guidance and embraced the JITI concept as part of my Lean Learning journey.

My next step was to write my study guide, so that's where I focused my information gathering. In true ITWEWWILL fashion, I used Microsoft Word because that's what I had available. I didn't concern myself with information about designing the cover or creating a sales page—without a completed study guide, those steps were irrelevant. By concentrating solely on acquiring the information needed for the task at hand, I was able to pour all my energy into crafting a high-quality product.

During the writing process, I sought out information on how to format text properly, create informative tables and charts, and add hyperlinks for easy navigation. These were the specific pieces of knowledge I needed to complete my current step, and I avoided the temptation to dive into unrelated topics.

Once the study guide was complete, I moved on to the next step: designing the book cover. I focused on finding the resources and information I needed to create an attractive and professional-looking cover.

After that was finished, it was time to create a sales page to help effectively convert visitors to my website into customers. From recommendations in the business community I was a part of, I quickly found my way to a book called *Moonlighting on the Internet* by Yanik Silver.

In the back of this book was a chapter on writing a sales page with a Mad Libs style template that you could copy with blank spaces to insert your own product name, features, benefits, and price point. It was the only chapter of this book that I read, and it served me perfectly for what I needed. And after the sales page was published, the JITI concept continued to guide me through the entire process of launching and fulfilling my product. In some cases the information I needed came from resources within the communities I was a part of, and other times, it was as simple as a Google search.

By focusing on one step at a time and gathering only the information required for that particular stage, I was able to maintain momentum and avoid getting overwhelmed. The resources and knowledge I needed were always available; I just didn't need to access them until the appropriate moment in my journey. This focused approach allowed me to create a better study guide than I initially thought possible. It was a powerful lesson in the effectiveness of seeking out Just-in-Time Information as part of the Lean Learning process.

With each completed step, I gained momentum and confidence, celebrating every mini-milestone while trusting that the path would unfold as long as I kept moving forward and seeking out the right information at the right time. As soon as I unlocked one stage, I was driven and ready to find the answers quickly so I could unlock the next, and the results spoke for themselves.

In October 2008, I launched the *LEED AP Walkthrough Study Guide* and generated a total of $7,908.55 in the first month. The revenue continued to grow, and I applied the same JITI concept to create an audiobook version of the book, too. Today, *Green*

Exam Academy still helps customers pass the LEED exam and has generated well over seven figures in its lifetime.

At SPI, we structure our courses using the same focused information approach. We've learned not to overwhelm students by providing all the information up front, instead encouraging them to concentrate on acquiring the knowledge needed for one lesson at a time. This format has helped us achieve completion rates of up to 37 percent, far surpassing the industry standard of 5 to 10 percent.

Dealing with FOMO

When you commit to Just-in-Time Information (JITI) and concentrate on the necessary information for your next action, you might encounter FOMO—the fear of missing out. This fear stems from the worry that by not scouring through various sources, you might miss something important. While this concern is natural, it's essential to recognize that FOMO acts more like a trap than a legitimate warning signal, leading to inaction or diverting you into unnecessary side quests.

The common advice in this situation is to just cut yourself off from everything that could possibly derail you. The problem is, going cold turkey is hard, and if you're like me and rely on platforms like email and use social media to connect with audiences and build rapport, then it's nearly impossible to avoid some sort of juicy information coming across your feed that looks interesting and may actually be useful, but just not right now. Plus, if I left social media, my wife and I wouldn't be able to share funny memes with each other anymore, and memes are one of our love languages.

Anyway, rather than letting FOMO steer you into a cycle of endless information gathering, which can stall your progress and overwhelm you, here's how to maintain focus and drive action:

1. **Implement a "For Later" system**: Utilize tools like Notion, Evernote, or ClickUp to create a "For Later" folder. Whenever you encounter interesting information that doesn't pertain to your current task, save it here. This method helps segregate nonurgent information and keeps your current workspace clutter-free, allowing you to concentrate on the task at hand. What's funny is 99 percent of the time, you'll never go back and look at your "For Later" folder—it's simply a way for you to move past the distraction and back into what you should be doing.

2. **Trust your chosen path**: Have confidence in the streamlined path you've selected. This trust minimizes second-guessing and reduces the urge to veer off course in search of more information.

3. **Set information boundaries**: Define clear boundaries about what type of information you need and when you need it. This helps filter out the noise and focus on what's truly necessary for the current phase of your project.

4. **Use FOMO as a checkpoint**: Instead of viewing FOMO negatively, use it as a checkpoint to reassess your current informational needs. Ask yourself, "Is this feeling pointing me toward something I genuinely need to know right now, or is it just a distraction?" In the beginning this takes a conscious effort; however, with enough practice it will become second nature.

5. **Embrace scheduled learning**: Allocate specific times for learning new information that might be useful later. This scheduled approach allows you to focus on immediate tasks while knowing there's a time set aside for broader learning, thereby easing FOMO. To discuss scheduled learning further, let's dive into a strategy that you may have heard of before, but with a little twist on it.

Time Blocking as a Verb

To fully harness the power of Lean Learning, it's crucial to dedicate specific blocks of time to focus on your next step. This is where the concept of time blocking comes into play, but it's more than just about scheduling blocks of time on your calendar.

You've probably heard of time blocking before. It's a time management technique that's been around for decades, but more recently it's been gaining popularity thanks to people like Cal Newport, author of *Deep Work* and *Digital Minimalism*.

At its core, time blocking is all about being intentional with how you structure your day. You take your schedule and divide it up into dedicated chunks of time. Each block is reserved for a specific task or set of related tasks that you need to tackle.

To make this really work, however, you have to go beyond mechanically adding blocks of time into your calendar—you have to adopt a time blocking mindset by focusing more on the verb than the noun. In other words, it's not time blocking because you've created a block of time in your calendar, but because you created a vaultlike space for you to focus, and your calendar blocks anything else from entering that space.

You want to be the Mandalorian who forges impenetrable Beskar armor to shield yourself from the distractions and interruptions of the world. Just as Beskar protects against blaster bolts and lightsaber strikes, your time blocking shields your focus, ensuring that you maintain control over your tasks and priorities. *This is the way.*

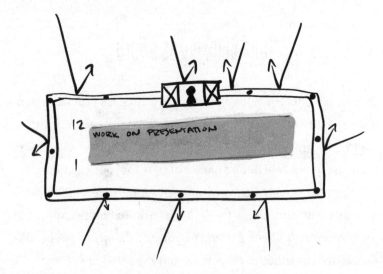

The key to time blocking is that during each block, you give your full attention to the work at hand. No multitasking and no distractions. Just you and the task, working together to make progress. Time blocking is the exact method I use to structure my own day, and having dedicated time on the calendar to do everything from work-related items to hobbies and even family time, I don't have to think about what is supposed to happen, when it's supposed to happen. Taking action toward your goals can only truly happen when you include that time in your calendar.

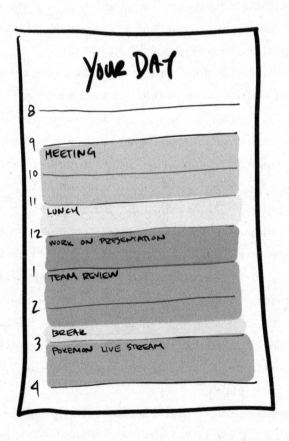

Unfortunately, this reads well on paper, but there's a common problem. I've experienced it, my students have experienced it, and chances are, you've experienced it, too. Just because you put something on the calendar doesn't mean it gets done.

Life happens. We get distracted. A notification interrupts our flow. The baby cries in the next room. Your dog barks at the doorbell. A kid needs to be picked up from school. Time blocking is perfect on paper, but difficult in practice, and as outside forces infiltrate our schedule, we have to move things around and sacrifice things that we had set out to do, and when that happens, guess which items tend to get crossed off first? The new inspirations we tried to make time for.

Daniel Kahneman has written about focus and the prevalence of distractions in our society today in his best-selling book *Thinking, Fast and Slow*. In his book, he shares multiple examples of how we can all miss certain things when we aren't looking for them, including the famous example of the gorilla experiment, also called the "selective attention test," where volunteers are told to keep track of how many times basketball players can be seen passing a basketball to each other in a circle. As you watch them pass the ball back and forth, trying to count the times, you may, as many people do, miss the fact that a person in a gorilla suit walks out and dances around while this is happening. Most people, not surprisingly, fail to see the gorilla. Kahneman explains that this is due to our own blindness. It's not just that we're "blind to the obvious," he writes, but that we're "blind to our own blindness."[1]

There's no avoiding distractions completely, but there are two actions you can take to immediately combat this frustration. The first comes from Cal Newport himself: schedule out your distractions. As Cal said on my show, "The reason scheduling your distraction helps is because all of the time outside of those scheduled distractions, your brain is still going to crave the quick hit. What you're doing now is resisting it by saying, 'Yeah, I'll give you that hit, but not for twenty more minutes when I've scheduled the time.' That's twenty minutes of your brain practicing being exposed to the desire for stimuli and not giving in."

The second action is to recommit and honor the time you've set aside for your new inspiration. Whether it's an hour a day or just thirty minutes per week—whatever it is, honor it. Practice following through on what you said you were going to do.

Remember: if it doesn't relate, eliminate.

Tackling Time Challenges

Now that we've learned how to give ourselves the best opportunity to dive into our actions, we must talk about what will inevitably happen to most who are venturing into new territory thanks to these new inspirations. You *will* face challenges and setbacks. It's not a matter of *if*, but *when*.

As you embark on your journey to pursue your newfound inspirations, you'll quickly realize that the path to success is rarely a straight line. There will be obstacles, detours, and moments when you feel like giving up. Boredom may even rear its head, tempting you to question your commitment. But here's the thing: these challenges, including boredom, are not roadblocks. They're opportunities for growth.

In the next chapter, we'll explore multiple strategies for pushing through these challenging moments and staying committed to your path, even when the excitement fades and boredom creeps in. But now, let's dive in and learn to navigate the ups and downs of pursuing your inspirations.

Anti-Champions

Wherever there are cheerleaders and champions, you will also find those who want to discourage you. I can't tell you how often I heard after I had been laid off, "When are you going to get a real job?"

This happened well into running my own successful business online. Many people will criticize and question what they don't understand, and that was certainly the case with me and many of my old coworkers and even some friends.

Some people couldn't believe that a person who was laid off from their job could create something better than what they had before. In many cases, when I told old friends from architecture what I was up to, the most common reaction I received was pity. They felt sorry for me, which wasn't exactly encouraging.

That was hard, and I eventually distanced myself from those negative voices. Because I had my champions, I didn't take their reactions to heart (but, I am human, and the words still hurt). What I eventually realized, though, was their words were a reflection of their own insecurities and disbelief in themselves. None of it had anything to do with me.

I once heard a story about a bucket of crabs. When you have a bucket of live crabs, you don't ever have to worry about any of those crabs crawling out: because as soon as one tries to escape, the other crabs use their pincers to pull the escaping crab back down.

We live in a world just like that, and our anti-champions are the crabs. They're especially active when we're trying to elevate ourselves, trying to do something special and make change for ourselves or others—there will always be those who try to pull us down. It's not that they want to hurt us; they just want to maintain the status quo, because it feels safe.

The "crabs in a bucket" concept was first coined by Filipina journalist and human rights activist Ninotchka Rosca. She argued that some people have a "crab mentality" where a person believes that if *they* can't have something, neither can anyone else. It's a form of scarcity thinking. There will always be people who try to pull us down for all kinds of reasons, because keeping others on their level is what feels good to them.

When you're going after your own dream, beware of the crabs. We all come from some "bucket" and whenever we try to go to the next level (to crawl out of where we came from), there will be people who try to stop us or talk us out of growth. These people see what we're trying to do and attempt to guide us in the opposite direction. They may even think they're helping. But the truth is others don't know what is best for us. Only we can know that for sure.

Sometimes, critics really do have wisdom to share, which is why we shouldn't completely shut out all voices. But once it becomes clear that someone is telling you that *you* can't do something because *they* were never able to do it, you know you're talking to a crab.

This is why it's so important to find our champions, because these people will help us stay on the path when others may come along and attempt to knock us off balance. It's one thing to find true north but another to keep moving in that direction, adjusting your course whenever you get off track. Your champions are your compass—hold on to them, and they'll help you reach your destination.

Hurt People Hurt People

When my son Keoni was ten years old, he wanted to start a YouTube channel. As a YouTuber myself, I was proud! I imagined him building an audience, learning to edit his own videos and tell great stories, maybe even learning how to generate some extra cash on the side to spend on Pokémon cards, or start a Roth IRA—both equally important. But on the other hand, I imagined a lot of the trolls and haters who could get to him. If we put his face on the internet, where all kinds of people could discover him and say all kinds of terrible things, that would not be okay. After a long discussion, my wife and I decided to start a YouTube account and let Keoni post videos on it, but only with our supervision, of course.

The rules were simple. He had to film his own videos, and edit them himself. He couldn't get any help from us. We were just there to ensure he was doing things safely, and a part of that was to be extremely honest and up front with him.

So I sat down with my son and taught him the lessons I'd

learned from criticism. "You know," I said, "I'd love for you to start a YouTube channel and you seem excited about it. But I need to tell you that it's going to invite people into your channel that might be hateful. They might share mean things and say hurtful words and try to take you down. They'll do this for all kinds of reasons. But just remember that hurt people hurt people. And when people say these things and try to tear somebody else down, it's usually because something else is happening in their life. It's not you, especially if you know that what you're doing is good and of value to people."

A couple months went by, and he created a few videos. On his channel, Keoni reviewed puzzles and did other fun and creative things like creating a Skee-Ball machine out of cardboard—a video that actually went a little viral with tens of thousands of views. It wasn't long before he came up to me one morning, and said, "Dad, somebody left a nasty comment on one of my videos."

I had told him to tell me the first time it happened. When he did, I went to the channel and checked the comment. All it said was: "Kill yourself."

I couldn't believe it. As a parent, I was filled with rage, so upset but also wanting to stay calm for my son. Waiting to see how my son felt, I asked him what he thought about the comment, and after thinking for a moment, he responded: "I hope they're okay."

That's when I started to cry. This lesson I had taught him about trolls had actually helped him understand one of the most important lessons in life, something that took me years to understand, and haters and trolls had almost made me quit a few times in my past.

These lessons about understanding why people behave the way they do are important. It will save you a lot of pain and frustration in life if you can more clearly see what is motivating a person, especially when they try to attack you.

As we are all on our own learning journeys, trying to level up in life, we will eventually encounter a critic. A hater. A bully. While we're trying to get better, to discover new things and improve our own lives, we have to remember that there will be people out there who want to tear us down.

But that's not what they really want. What they want is to be understood, to be told that they're okay. And we may not be able to do that for them. But we can receive the gift of their criticism, quietly thanking them from afar for whatever it taught us, and sending them empathy.

Even if they are trying to hurt us, I find that this is still the best, healthiest response. Why? Because it feels better.

You Can't Say "*Yes*" to Everything

A few years back, I had the pleasure of interviewing Paul Jarvis, a designer and entrepreneur who is an incredible example of the wisdom and power in staying focused on our original intentions and opting out of the more-is-better mindset.

When Paul started his own design business, he quickly found himself at a crossroads. His work was making such a big impact for his clients, they kept recommending Paul to their own networks, and he had no shortage of opportunity to take on more clients. He could have followed the conventional path of expansion, hiring more people and taking on more clients to fuel growth.

But Paul recognized this approach would come at the cost of the very things he valued most: his freedom, his enjoyment of work, and his ability to deliver high-quality results. Instead, he made the conscious choice to prioritize these elements over the temptation of unbridled growth.

"I never wanted to be in a position," he told me during the interview, "where [I] had so many expenses and so much overhead [that] it had to be just *yes* to everything."

He also never wanted to make business decisions that took him away from doing the things he liked, like sitting at his desk and writing. Paul knew the power of *no* and embraced it so that he could say *yes* to what he truly loved, growing a company of one that was focused on doing better work instead of simply getting bigger.

This decision to opt out of the bigger-is-better mentality allowed Paul to create a business that truly aligned with his values and goals. By being selective about the clients he worked with and charging more for his services, he was able to grow his profits without sacrificing his autonomy or the joy he found in his craft.

As my own business started to flourish, and more opportunities came into the picture, I was indeed saying *yes* to more than I should. Paul helped me slow down and be more conscious about where I was taking my business, and how I wanted to get there. I'm not a company of one like Paul, but I do have a company of fun. Okay, that's a bit corny, but it's true.

The Joy of Opting Out

As we progress on our own learning journeys, we will face critical moments of decision where what we do next impacts our success (or lack thereof). The momentum of our progress and the confidence we gain from these efforts can be intoxicating, leading us to take on more than we originally planned. We may find ourselves juggling multiple projects, adding new layers of complexity to our work, and stretching ourselves too thin, all in the pursuit of more.

This is a common trap many of my students, particularly in my podcasting courses, fall into. They set out to start one show, but as they dive in and discover it's not as hard as they thought, they decide to launch a second one. Before they know it, they're managing two or three podcasts at once, adding a video version of each, then running multiple YouTube channels and cutting clips for social media to repurpose their work into smaller bite-sized chunks.

At first, it feels fun and exciting to be working on so many things. But eventually? The end result is a feeling of exhaustion and being overwhelmed, as well as a loss of focus on their original goals. After a while, they feel like there's no catching up and they have to let it all go.

The key to avoiding this trap is to remember why you started your learning journey in the first place. What were the core values, passions, and objectives that sparked your desire to learn and grow? By staying connected to these original intentions, you can more easily navigate the temptations of expansion and opt out of opportunities that don't align with your true priorities.

How do you know what your values and priorities are or *should* be? That's easy. Take a look at your schedule. I always say I can tell who a person is by looking at their calendar. What you value is not what you say you value—it's what you make time for.

So the first step in figuring out what your priorities are is to look at how you spend your time on a daily, weekly, and monthly basis.

Then, ask yourself, is this how you want to spend your time or energy? Or is something misaligned? How, if you could wave a magic wand, would you spend your days? The answer to that question is the beginning of what truly matters—to *you*.

You don't have to have this all figured out yet. But if you are consistently doing things that are not important to you and/or not making room for the things that are, then it's time for some serious self-reflection.

We know what our core values are when we pay attention to where we spend our time and who we spend it with. If taking on a new opportunity will compete with those priorities, we need to admit that we don't really value what we say we do. Or, we need to stay focused on what matters most to us and let the chips fall where they may.

This isn't to say new challenges are bad. There may be times when taking on additional projects or responsibilities serves your ultimate goals. The crucial thing, though, is to approach these decisions mindfully, with a clear understanding of what you're willing to trade and what you're not. By cultivating a joy of opting out, you give yourself permission to say *no* to the things that don't serve your core purposes, even if they seem appealing at the time.

When we say *no* to the nonessentials, we create space for what truly lights us up and allows us to do our best work. Like Paul Jarvis, we can build lives and businesses that prioritize quality, enjoyment, and alignment over relentless growth for growth's sake.

As you continue on your learning journey, remember that protecting your focus and staying true to your original intentions is a powerful act of self-preservation. Don't be afraid to opt out of the noise and distractions that threaten to pull you off course. Embrace the freedom and fulfillment that come from knowing what matters to you and having the courage to pursue it.

In the next chapter, we'll explore how to translate this clarity into focused action. By combining the joy of opting out with one of the most powerful steps you can take on your journey, you'll be well equipped to navigate the exciting challenges and opportunities that lie ahead on your learning journey.

5.

Voluntary Force Functions

"If the road is easy, you're likely going the wrong way."

—Terry Goodkind

W e've all faced high-pressure situations that force us to learn quickly, not because we wanted to—but because we had to. Whether it's cramming for a crucial exam, racing to meet a demanding deadline at work, or having to get your life back in order after getting laid off, we've all experienced moments that require us to get out of our comfort zone and figure things out, *fast*.

Yet, reflecting on these experiences in life, I recognize that for me they were largely reactive. I didn't choose these high-pressure moments as much as they often just came with the territory of whatever new thing I was doing, or was forced to do. While I certainly grew and developed because of these challenging situations, I also started to wonder: *Would I be able to learn new things faster if I purposefully put myself in higher-pressure situations?*

That question is the essence of this chapter.

I practice what I like to call "Voluntary Force Functions." By deliberately placing myself in challenging circumstances, circumstances that require me to step up, I increase the likelihood that I will follow through on my commitment and achieve my goals. These chosen environments catalyze rapid learning and personal growth. They are incredibly powerful when it comes to Lean Learning, so powerful, in fact, that Voluntary Force Functions have become my go-to "hack" for *speedrunning* skill acquisition (that's gamer speak, by the way—speedrunning is the process of racing through a game as quickly as possible so that you can get to the end in record time).

When we choose to opt into situations where we have to do the thing instead of just waiting around for it, we can harness a temporary and strategic stressor for life-changing transformation. This is about stepping into growth deliberately; it's about moving from being a passive participant in your life to an active architect of your own development.

There is a delicate balance, however, between placing yourself in an elevated-pressure situation for growth and learning and purposefully overwhelming yourself to the brink of burnout or breakdown. So be careful here.

As an entrepreneur and advisor to several start-up companies, I've seen firsthand what a self-inflicted challenge can do to a person's mental and physical health.

Please understand that a Voluntary Force Function is not about "hustle" or having to sacrifice happiness and comfort to endure pain like it's a rite of passage to success. Instead, these scenarios are about purposefully extending yourself just beyond your comfort zone, for a measured amount of time, to experience personal and professional development.

Voluntary Force Functions are designed to create intentional constraints that compel action. They are the chosen conditions that make a desired behavior nearly inevitable. These functions excel at long-term habit formation or to overcome procrastination on daunting tasks, serving as structural changes to our environment and routine that promote ongoing success.

Ever since I was three years old, I've been catching fresh and saltwater fish using hundreds of different methods, but there was one bait I could never figure out: the *jig*. A jig is a weighted hook that's usually furnished with a plastic skirt to give it some movement, and when a fish bites it, a jig can lead to an intense and exhilarating hook set—the fish attracted to jigs are usually bigger, too.

I've always wanted to learn to fish with a jig but had zero confidence with it. Every time I tied a jig on to try it out, I'd always revert back to the baits I was more confident with, like a crankbait or plastic worm. One day, though, when I was getting ready to go back out on the water, I followed the Voluntary Force Function practice and purposefully left every single bait at home except one—the jig.

While on the water for six hours that day, I had no choice but to figure it out, and every time I wanted to go back and try something else, I couldn't. I was forced to learn how to use the jig. Nearing the end of the day, I finally hooked a fish and that was all I needed. My confidence grew after that and no longer could I tell myself, "I'm never going to catch one doing this."

I've since caught some of my biggest largemouth bass—including my personal best—using a jig. That's the power of a Voluntary Force Function.

Now, rather than just give you a menu of how these force functions work—a menu that would be as extensive as the one from the Cheesecake Factory (I swear, they are not sponsoring this book, but they should be!)—I'm instead going to give you a list of ingredients to use, so that you can cook up your own.

After a decade of intentional practice, and after guiding thousands of students through their own growth experiences, I'm going to share my five-part recipe for the most impactful kind of pressure you could ask for. When you decide to cook one up for yourself, you can change the spice level to suit your own tastes and needs. But hopefully my approach will help you get started.

Before I share with you my recipe, though, let me show you an example of the finished product: one of my first, and most transformational, Voluntary Force Functions ever—the first time I ever spoke in public.

My Most Transformational Force Function

In 2011, my new podcast had become the #1 business podcast on iTunes (before it became Apple Podcasts), and the demand for my time and attention grew exponentially. My inbox was getting bombarded daily with partnership opportunities from companies, podcasters who wanted me on their show, and listeners and readers who wanted my help.

Keeping up with my emails was hard, and I ended up having to hire someone full-time just to manage the inbox. There was one type of inquiry, however, that was super easy to manage. Every time I saw one make its way into my inbox, I immediately redirected it to the archive.

No, it wasn't for spam.

It was any request to have me come speak at a live event.

I said *no* to every single opportunity where I was asked to speak—but not because I was trying to stay focused. In fact, speaking onstage was a huge opportunity that aligned with my goals to help more people and become more of an authority figure in the online business world.

I said *no* because I was deathly afraid to speak in front of a crowd.

Most people fear public speaking, and I was definitely in that group—but I was an extreme case. Despite knowing public speaking would be hugely beneficial for my business and personal growth, just the thought of getting up in front of people and delivering a presentation gave me hot flashes and cold sweats. Seriously. It terrified me.

In the middle of that year, however, my friend Philip Taylor (aka "PT") called and asked for a huge favor. He wanted me to deliver the closing keynote at his inaugural event, The Financial Blogger Conference (FinCon), in Schaumburg, Illinois, that August.

Oh yeah, it was already July.

For anyone else, it would have been an immediate *no*. But PT needed help, and he was my friend. The scheduled keynote speaker had just bailed on him at the last minute due to a serious personal emergency, and I knew how much this event meant to him. I also knew that if I was ever going to conquer my fear of public speaking, this was my chance.

So, despite my fears, I said *yes*. I volunteered as tribute.

What happened next was transformational. After the initial shock of what I'd just agreed to do had worn off, I immediately started to put in the work. In true ITWEWWILL fashion, I reached out to a couple of friends—aka *champions*—who had spoken on stages before, and asked for their advice. One of them told me to pick up a book, *Stand and Deliver* by Dale Carnegie. Just the information I needed, *just in time*.

Knowing every *yes* is a *no* to something else, my trivial work got pushed aside for the time remaining before the event, and my gaming console took a much needed break. I dove right in. It was a high-pressure, high-stakes situation, and that's what drove me to stay focused.

I had less than thirty days to prepare, and by intentionally putting myself in this situation, I had just created the perfect conditions for a powerful transformation.

The looming deadline, high personal stakes (I didn't want to let my friend down, after all), and the potential upside all fueled my motivation. The inherent challenge of the task pushed me outside of my comfort zone, and the opportunity to prepare gave me the tools I needed to succeed. It was a Voluntary Force Function.

When the big day arrived, I was a ball of nerves. I still remember pacing through the hallways of the convention center hours before my talk, even getting lost once because although I had arrived two days before, I had spent most of my time in the hotel room practicing in front of the mirror. I even practiced with my suit coat on, because I believed it would help me get a better sense of what it would be like to do the real thing.

I was ready.

At 4 p.m. on the last day of the event, PT introduced me. On my way up to the stage, he handed me the clicker to advance the slides, and after the applause died down, I looked up at the audience through the bright lights and . . . *froze.*

I had forgotten what to say. Every word of it. I couldn't remember anything.

To buy myself some time, I asked the audience to give my friend a round of applause—after they had *just* finished applauding for me. Then I kept stalling, talking about how great an experience the event was and, in my head, also realizing that if I bombed the keynote, it would be the last impression of the event anyone had and could possibly ruin my career forever, and also that my friend Philip Taylor would get bad reviews for his event, and it would never happen again and I'd end up naked in a ditch somewhere and—at least, that's what was going through my head at the time. Then I remembered where to begin, and I started the talk.

After that, something took over me. I started to go on autopilot. Apparently, all my preparation had paid off. The presentation was in full swing now, and it began to feel like an out-of-body experience. And then, almost as quickly as it had begun, it was over only twenty-four minutes later.

I had just survived my first public speech.

The audience cheered, and I looked over at PT to see how I had done. He had a huge smile on his face, and I knew I hadn't let him down. I knew I hadn't let myself down, either.

At that moment, even though I had been scared, I was proud of myself for getting up there, for doing it. My presentation was far from perfect. It was, after all, my first speech! Reluctantly looking back at the recording later that year, I saw that I had paced back and forth across the stage a lot, stumbled over a few words, and skipped an entire section. I was even holding a water bottle in my hand the entire time and never even drank from it!

But I also surprised myself. Unscripted, I added in jokes that made the audience laugh. The content kept them engaged, and after the event was over, I had a line of people outside the ballroom wanting to meet me. Many of them complimented me and were surprised to hear it was my first time speaking onstage.

Since then, I've spoken on more than 300 stages around the world, and I am now getting paid for speaking, which I never thought would happen. In total, I've generated over half a million dollars in revenue just from presentations and keynotes—and I even started hosting my own live events, too. Not bad for a guy who used to avoid every opportunity to get on a stage!

Recently, in a full circle moment, PT and his son Drew, who collects Pokémon cards, attended my event Card Party. Card Party brings thousands of Pokémon fans together with their favorite Pokémon creators from all around the world, and when I saw my friend at the event, I nearly broke down in tears. A lot of what I have to be thankful for is a direct result of the opportunity *he* gave me back in 2011. I'm glad I said *yes*.

You never know what can happen when you put yourself in the right place where you are forced to learn and grow.

The Recipe for an Effective Voluntary Function

Looking back, it's clear that saying yes to PT's invitation was one of the best decisions I ever made. By agreeing to take on that challenge, I inadvertently created the right condition for a rapid transformation. All the key ingredients of an effective Voluntary Force Function were there. And I want to share those with you now.

You don't need all of the following to experience a meaningful breakthrough, but the more you can incorporate, the better.

Let's break down each element of an effective Voluntary Force Function.

1. A Leap of Faith Moment

What exactly is a "Leap of Faith Moment"? It's that pulse-racing moment when you decide to turn "someday" into "starting now." For me, that came when I said *yes* to the invitation to speak onstage, despite my stomach twisting in knots. It was a shift from hesitation to action, a commitment to facing my fears head-on.

For you, I'm sure it'll look slightly different.

Remember that this leap of faith you take is not about reckless abandon. It's a deeply considered decision that launches you out of the planning phase and into action. It's about trusting your ability to rise to the challenge and that you have the resources and resilience to see it through. Here are a few examples to illustrate what these moments can look like:

- If you're hoping to learn to speak a certain language, your Leap of Faith Moment is when you enroll in that class, or book your ticket to another country.
- If you're looking to step away from your 9–5 job, after you've prepared yourself, it's the moment you put in your two-weeks' notice.
- If you're inspired to run your first marathon, it's the moment you register for the next race.

Each of these moments marks a significant turning point, and when you commit to a Leap of Faith Moment, you're not just hoping to land safely on the other side; you're activating all the resources at your disposal to ensure that you give yourself the best chance to succeed.

2. A Time-Locked Commitment

A hard deadline transforms intention into action. When I agreed to deliver that keynote, I wasn't just saying yes to an opportunity—I was committing to a specific, immovable date. This wasn't a goal with a flexible timeline; it was a commitment that created a compelling sense of urgency. Suddenly, there was no room for fear or procrastination. The fixed date on the calendar forced me to focus, to prioritize my preparations, and push through my hesitation.

The key to a time-locked commitment is to treat your deadlines as nonnegotiable. People set goals for themselves, or deadlines, only to push them back repeatedly. I see this pattern again and again among my students. Although I understand life can interrupt our plans, I also know that when a deadline truly cannot be moved, we somehow find a way to meet it.

The easiest way to solidify your commitment, if it's not baked into the leap of faith you've already made, is to put it on your calendar—but not in the way you probably think you should.

Ask a champion of yours (ideally, a mentor) to create the deadline on their calendar and invite you to the event. You won't be able to move it, and you'll know it's on the calendar of the person who is holding you accountable. It will be harder to get out of, which means you are more likely to follow through.

3. High Stakes

The stakes were significant but not paralyzing when I accepted the invitation to speak at FinCon. My professional reputation and friendship with PT were on the line, heightening my desire to excel. This type of pressure, when kept within manageable limits, can transform fear into a motivator rather than a hindrance.

It's vital to keep in perspective what "high stakes" means. We imagine the worst: irreparably damaging our reputation or making a mistake so severe that recovery is impossible. But by realistically assessing the risks and asking ourselves, "What's the worst that could happen?" we uncover the truth—our fears are exaggerated.

When setting up your own Voluntary Force Functions, aim for stakes that push you out of your comfort zone but remain within a threshold that promotes action. This might involve making a promise to a mentor, risking a sum of money, or something else. Not doing it needs to hurt a little— but not be so terrifying you're afraid to risk it.

Find that sweet spot where the risk is enough to keep you driven, but not so daunting it overwhelms you. Author Steven Pressfield suggests that fear is not always an enemy; it emerges precisely when we are about to do something meaningful, something that matters. Let that guide your efforts.

High stakes should motivate, not debilitate.

4. Meaningful Challenge

Choosing to tackle my fear of speaking wasn't a random decision—it was strategically aligned with both my personal growth and professional ambitions. Mastering this skill wasn't just about overcoming a fear, it was about discovering new ways to reach more people and make a more meaningful impact in the world.

When designing your own Voluntary Force Functions, it's crucial to select challenges that are not only difficult but also deeply meaningful to you and align with your values. Consider the following:

- **Personal resonance:** Choose a challenge that resonates with your core values and aligns with your long-term goals. Whether it's confronting a long-held fear, mastering a complex skill, or making a significant impact in your community, the challenge should feel profoundly important to you.

- **Motivation through meaning:** The more the challenge matters to you personally, the stronger your drive will be to engage with it and succeed. This connection turns a daunting task into a compelling mission, infusing your efforts with purpose and determination.

- **Assessing impact:** Ask yourself, what are the potential outcomes of conquering this challenge? How will overcoming this particular hurdle enhance your life or career? Understanding the tangible benefits can provide additional motivation and clarify the challenge's value.

By ensuring your challenges are meaningful, you're not just setting goals, you're crafting milestones that reflect your deepest aspirations and desired impact. This alignment makes the journey as rewarding as the destination, ensuring sustained effort and engagement.

5. Rewards on the Other End

When I stepped onstage at FinCon, it wasn't just about overcoming a personal hurdle. It was also about unlocking new horizons. That first talk was the gateway to a series of enriching experiences to come in my speaking career.

After that event, I hired a coach to mentor me through my next talks. And I had many more opportunities to step onstage and share a message with an audience. But had I not taken that first step, none of it would have been possible. Similarly, once I'd crossed that threshold, I had to keep raising the stakes, keep stepping through new doorways.

This is key to the Lean Learning process: you have to keep going. The small wins are only significant when you leverage them for larger wins down the line.

In designing your own Voluntary Force Functions, first think beyond the immediate challenge—but then zoom out and consider what else it could make possible. Ask yourself: "What new opportunities could this open up for me, if I did?"

Perhaps, mastering public speaking could lead to leadership roles or more keynote opportunities. My conquering a personal fitness goal could inspire a business idea or health blog. Or, maybe like me, a weird obsession with trading cards could open up a whole new career for you. Consider the doors your current challenge might unlock, but don't limit yourself to what you think is possible. Just be open to what could come. You never know what bigger skills your next pursuit will help you build.

Try to keep the bigger picture in mind, even if you don't know what the future holds. Think of how mastering *this* fear or *that* skill could catapult you into all kinds of arenas, enhancing your life and career. This broader perspective can serve as a powerful motivator, especially when obstacles arise. You're not just doing this for today; you're doing it for what could come tomorrow.

By viewing your current challenge as a stepping-stone to greater things, you reinforce the value of pushing through, ensuring that each step forward not only brings personal growth but propels you to broader opportunities. It's not just about what you achieve by conquering the challenge—it's about what conquering the challenge allows you to achieve next.

Examples of Voluntary Force Functions

To help guide you further, I've included a few examples below of Voluntary Force Functions that hit all five ingredients from above:

Voluntary Force Function	Leap of Faith Moment	Time-Locked Commitment	High Stakes	Meaningful Challenge	Rewards on the Other End
Learning a New Language	Book a trip to Japan for 3 months from now.	Arrival date in Japan.	Navigating a foreign country without proficiency.	Connecting with Japanese culture and people.	Potential business opportunities and relationships in Japan. Explore for a potential move.
Starting a Business	Quit your job to focus on your business full-time.	Date of resignation.	Financial security and professional reputation.	Pursuing your passion and creating something of your own.	The freedom and fulfillment of entrepreneurship.
Running a Marathon	Register for a marathon 6 months from now.	Race day.	Physical and mental challenge of completing 26.2 miles.	Proving to yourself that you can achieve a major athletic goal.	Increased confidence, discipline, and physical fitness.

All right, you're almost ready to put together all these elements in the recipe I just provided. But before I let you cook (that's a Gen Z pun for the younger ones reading this book), let me ask you a question: *Do you think it's better to share your goals with others, or not?* The science-based answer I'm about to share may surprise you.

The Truth About Sharing Your Goals

When it comes to Voluntary Force Functions, most people believe simply announcing their intentions publicly, like on social media, will help keep them accountable and act as a force function. However, research suggests this approach can backfire.

In a 2009 study conducted by Peter Gollwitzer, a professor of psychology at New York University, researchers found that when individuals shared their goals with others, they reported feeling closer to achieving them, even though they hadn't made any actual progress. The act of sharing the goal itself made them feel a premature sense of accomplishment, which in turn reduced their motivation to put in the work required to actually achieve the goal.[1]

Gollwitzer and his colleagues concluded that when someone notices your goal, that recognition is a reward that may cause you to reduce your own efforts. In other words, the satisfaction you get from having others *see* you as "the type of person who would achieve that goal" can trick your brain into thinking you've already done it. This, then, reduces the pressure to finish the goal (since in your mind, you've already done it), and as a result, you wind up quitting.

So we have to be intentional about how we share our goals. Newer research from Ohio State University in 2019 suggests there may be a right way to do it, though. In a series of experiments, researchers at Ohio State found that people tend to be more committed to their goals after they share them with someone they perceive as "higher status," or whose opinions they respect.[2]

In one study, college students who shared their target goals with a doctoral-level student were more likely to reach their goals, while those who shared with someone they believed to be a community college student did not perform better. Similarly, students who shared their ambitious grade goals with someone of higher status tended to be more committed to their grades by the end of the semester.

The key to success, according to lead author Howard Klein, is sharing your goal with a higher-up. This does more than hold you accountable; it makes you more motivated because you care what this person thinks of you. It's using social recognition to your advantage—this, too, is a form of Voluntary Force Function.

So, while sharing your goals on social media may not be the most effective strategy, selectively disclosing those goals to individuals whose opinions you value and respect could provide the right kind of motivation and accountability to help you stay committed. This is a role that your champion mentors can take, as well as other champions you might have access to in communities you're a part of.

In our entrepreneurial community at SPI, we encourage our users to share their intentions with our Experts in Residence (EIRs), i.e., established businessowners we've partnered with who are there to specifically help our community members and hold them accountable. When you share your goals with the right people, you increase your chances of achieving the right results. Like so many things in life, it's not so much whether you do this, but how—and with whom.

Designing Your Own Voluntary Force Functions

Now that we've explored the key components and have seen some examples of effective Voluntary Force Functions, it's time to start designing your own transformative challenges.

Start by identifying an area where you feel stuck or know you need to grow. Ask yourself, "What scares me but also excites me? What would challenge me in a meaningful way?"

Look for opportunities that align with your values and aspirations. Chances are, you already have an idea of a Voluntary Force Function you can initiate, and if you're like most people, it's something you've already had in mind for a while, perhaps even before picking up this book.

If you're struggling to come up with something, this is where asking a champion in your life can help a lot. They may be able to see something or discover a way for you to grow that's right in front of you, and if you have a personal mentor, now's the time to ask them for help.

Then, consider how you can incorporate the key elements we discussed above:

1. Choose your Leap of Faith Moment and commit to the challenge.

2. Set a time-locked commitment that creates urgency.

3. Ensure the stakes are high enough to be motivating but not paralyzing.

4. Choose a challenge that is meaningful to you and aligned with your goals.

5. Keep the rewards on the other end in mind as motivation.

Remember: the goal is to stretch outside your comfort zone, not overwhelm yourself. Start with a challenge that feels manageable but scares you a little. Then, as you build your Voluntary Force Function muscle, you can gradually increase the intensity.

And don't forget to take it just one challenge at a time.

Finally, celebrate each win along the way, no matter how small. Every challenge you conquer is proof of your resilience, capability, and growth. Use these victories as fuel for bigger and bolder challenges in the future.

By intentionally designing Voluntary Force Functions, you give yourself the power to accelerate your own transformation. You create the conditions for rapid growth and open up new realms of possibility. So take that leap of faith, embrace the challenge, and watch yourself soar to new heights. Your potential is limitless.

(If you'd like to watch my first presentation at FinCon in 2011, I have a link to it on the book site, along with the other resources mentioned in this chapter, at LeanLearningBook.com.)

6.

Persist or Pivot?

"Life is not a journey you want to make on autopilot."

—Paula Rinehart

Life is full of crossroads—moments when we must decide whether to continue on our current path or take a new direction. These decisions confront us when we've invested time, energy, and passion into our pursuits, making them especially daunting. Whether it's sticking with a project that isn't progressing as expected, or considering a shift in career after years in the same field, the question remains: Should I persist, or is it time to pivot?

This chapter explores that critical decision-making process. The choice is seldom clear-cut. It's not just about measuring success or acknowledging failure; it's about deeply understanding our goals, our methods, and ourselves. Like a navigator at sea deciding to adjust the sails or chart a new course, we must assess our position frequently and make informed decisions based on both the conditions around us and our destination.

It makes me wonder what would have happened if I had never been laid off from my job. Would I have become a project manager, maybe even started my own architectural practice? Would I have eventually quit my job, anyway, and become an entrepreneur, regardless? Most importantly, would I have ever beat George at golf?

It's impossible to know for sure, but what I do know is that pivotal moment in 2008 forced me to reassess my life and make a conscious decision regarding what to do next. And that, of course, changed everything.

My story is not unlike that of Brian Luebben. Brian was a top performer at a Fortune 500 sales organization, earning a substantial salary in his mid-twenties. He reached the pinnacle of success in corporate America only to realize he had climbed the wrong mountain. The life Brian had built for himself was not the one he actually wanted, which is not uncommon these days. But what he did next *was* rare.

Brian decided to start his own business, leaving behind the golden handcuffs of the corporate C-suite and pursuing his dream. Since 2022, he has traveled the world, sharing what he's learning about real estate, entrepreneurship, and replacing a life of hustle and grind with steady, predictable cash flow.

Brian chose to reassess his life, which was smart. I was forced to reassess mine, which was lucky. In the end, we both made crucial pivots that changed everything. You might be at a similar point in your journey where your current focus feels less fulfilling. Or maybe the results aren't what you expected. Perhaps new opportunities are calling or external circumstances have shifted, making you question your next steps. Should you keep pushing through, or is it time to pivot?

How you answer that question affects everything.

Or maybe things are going really well. If that's the case, it can be tempting to ride the wave and see where it takes you. But by taking the time to analyze your progress and identify the key drivers of your success, you can make strategic decisions to optimize your efforts, allocate resources more effectively, and capitalize on the momentum you've already built.

But when it comes to personal growth and achievement, autopilot is the enemy of progress. It's only by consciously re-assessing our path that we can ensure that we're steering toward our goals and making the most of our time and energy. Just as a sailor checks their compass and adjusts course, we, too, must learn to reevaluate our direction and make intentional choices about our next steps.

This chapter is about understanding when to stay the course and when to chart a new route. It will equip you with the tools you need to conduct a simple self-assessment, gather valuable feedback from those around you, and make informed decisions about your direction. But before we delve into whether to pivot or persist, it's crucial to revisit and reinforce the foundational element of any decision-making process: your *why*.

The Power of a Personal Why

You might be familiar with Simon Sinek, the author and motiva-tional speaker who is best known for popularizing the concept of "Start with Why." In his influential TED Talk (which is where I and millions of others were first introduced to this idea), Sinek argues that the most inspiring and successful leaders and organizations are those that focus first and foremost on their purpose, cause, or belief—their "why"—rather than on what they do or how they do it.

You and I, however, are not just companies or organizations. We're people. Human beings with inspirations that lead us into new and exciting parts of our lives. The values we possess, our own personal *whys*, become both the lights that illuminate our paths and the lighthouses that warn us of danger. In other words, it's not enough to start with *why*—we have to stick with it.

This is illustrated in the lives of Shane and Jocelyn Sams, whose entrepreneurial journey was not just about changing careers but about reshaping their lives to align with their most important priorities. For the Samses, their "why" emerged from a critical and emotional moment, one that any parent would absolutely dread.

One day during the summer of 2012, Shane Sams was out riding his lawn mower, listening to a podcast. Before he finished cutting the grass, Shane turned off the mower, burst into the kitchen where his wife, Jocelyn, was sitting, and told her that he had an idea that would change their lives. What *was* the phrase that caused this brainstorm? Two words: *passive income*.

It was the beginning of a new direction for them that would take many months—and a near-family tragedy—to unfold. As teachers working in rural Kentucky, Shane and Jocelyn epitomized what many would describe as the quintessential American Dream. Shane was a passionate U.S. History teacher and football coach, and Jocelyn was a beloved elementary school librarian. Together, they were living a comfortable existence with a seemingly secure path ahead of them. But their predictable trajectory took a sharp turn when a disturbing incident involving their three-year-old son not only challenged their day-to-day lives but also their future outlook on life.

One day, when Shane was dropping off their son at nursery school, not long after that experience of riding the lawn mower, his son refused to go inside, even started kicking and screaming in protest. Shane had little patience for this, because he had to make it to school on time to teach his first class. But his son insisted, yelling, "No daddy, no daddy, she *scares* me."

This stopped Shane in his tracks. When he asked his boy why he was afraid, Shane's son told him about some abusive incidents involving one of the employees at the nursery school.

Shane, of course, was horrified. There was no way he was going to leave his son there that day or any other day. But he also had a class to teach and couldn't get ahold of his wife, who was already at work, so he dropped his son off with a friend, drove to school, and spoke with his boss.

At school, Shane explained what had happened and asked if someone could cover his classes for the day so that he could figure things out at home. But because his son wasn't in "immediate danger," the supervisor told Shane, "I know your son needs you, but your job needs you, too, and you're gonna have to handle your personal problems after work."

Shane skipped his classes anyway, and went to get his son. On the way, he started feeling angry—but not at anyone else. At that moment, he wasn't mad at his boss or the person who had been hurting his boy. That would, of course, be normal and natural. Shane was upset with himself, disappointed in himself for living this life. It wasn't the kind of life he wanted for his family, and he knew that he had to make some changes—fast.

This pivotal moment marked the beginning of Shane and Jocelyn's entrepreneurial journey, highlighting not only what mattered most to them, but revealing the gaps in their abilities to fulfill their own values. It set them on a direction headed toward that dream of "passive income." Shane had heard about it on a podcast and now was determined to make it reality. He later reflected, "I realized I needed to create a life where, when my family needed me, I could be there without hesitation." He had spent too long tethering himself to other people's goals and ambitions; and now, it was time to put his family first.

Shane and Jocelyn built a life of freedom for themselves and their children, starting with some membership websites and other online programs. Eventually, they both quit their jobs and launched several businesses, including an online resource to help football coaches and an online resource for school librarians. Later, they started a podcast called *Flipped Lifestyle* to share more of their journey, and they have since gone on to earn millions of dollars and speak all over the world.

They now teach others to do what they have done: to reclaim their freedom and make the most of their lives.

I'm grateful to have been not just a spectator of this couple's journey but to have played a small role in it. It was my podcast, in fact, that helped Shane discover what was possible in the world of online business and that you don't need to create something that changes the whole world—just *somebody's* world—to build more freedom in your own life. Football coaches and school librarians were lucky to have their attention. More than that, though, I've been able to stay connected with the Samses over the years, and as I continue to watch their adventure unfold, one thing remains clear: their *why* guides their way.

Recently, Shane's speaking business started to grow. For a while, he had a team of nearly a dozen people working with him, and he was traveling all over the world several times a month. But suddenly, he stopped. After self-assessing and soliciting external feedback, it became clear that Shane had veered too far off course from his original goal. He wasn't seeing his family as much, and although his kids are much older and more independent now, he didn't want to use that as an excuse for losing his freedom to connect with his family whenever he wanted. That was, after all, what this was all about. He realized that these are the years to devote whatever time he and Jocelyn have left with their children before they become adults and start independent lives of their own. Once again, the Samses committed to what was most important to them, what got them started as entrepreneurs in the first place—their family.

This time, there was no "daycare moment," just a conscious check-in to reevaluate and pivot toward what mattered most. Speaking of daycare, that center soon went under investigation, and was shut down. When I asked Shane permission to use his and his wife's story in this book, he told me the decision they made to get clear on their "why" and change everything paid off in all aspects of their life. He told me sometimes, at crucial moments, you've got to make tough calls, turning left when everyone else is telling you to go right. But when you do these things for the right reasons, there's always something better waiting for you on the other side. To quote Shane, "there's power in the pivot." What could pivoting make possible for you?

Why, Though?

No matter where you're at in your journey, it's vital to periodically step back and reconnect with your original motivations. This connection to your foundational "why"—the spark that set you on this path—serves as the beacon that guides you through confusion and gives life back to your commitment. As someone who mentors several students, I see firsthand how easy it is to get absorbed in the day-to-day tasks and lose sight of the bigger picture. A part of my role as mentor is to point that out, because sometimes, taking a quick moment to remember our "why" is all we need to get back on track.

The "why" really does lead the way.

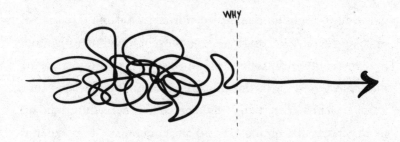

Reconnecting with your "why" is crucial, especially when you find yourself at a crossroads or facing significant decisions. In these moments, it's essential to step back and reflect on the journey—from where you started to where you are now—to ensure you remain aligned with your original motivations. However, you don't need to wait for a crisis or a major decision point to engage in this valuable reflection.

To make this process a regular part of your growth, I recommend setting aside fifteen minutes each month for a Why Focused Introspection, or Why-FI for short, because without that connection to your purpose, your progress might start to, dare I say . . . lag.

Dad jokes for the win.

Rather than tell you exactly how often you should check in, I'm going to make this easy for you, because remember that you just need to know the next action step that will help you. And that action step is this: schedule a one-hour "Self-Assessment Session" on your calendar within the next two weeks.

That's it. This block of time should be treated as a sacred space, free from distraction and interruption. Find a quiet, comfortable location where you can focus entirely on this process. If you're ambitious and ready to start this process sooner rather than later, schedule this hour tomorrow.

During your session, spend fifteen to twenty minutes reflecting on each of the topics listed below. This framework showcases the three areas of reflection I take myself and my students through during our evaluations.

1. **Progress:** How far have you come since starting this journey? What milestones have you achieved, and what challenges have you overcome?

2. **Passion:** Does this path still ignite your enthusiasm and motivation? Do you feel energized and excited when working toward your goal, or has your passion started to wane? What specific activities light you up, and what specific activities seem like a drag?

3. **Purpose:** Is this journey still aligned with your core values, beliefs, and long-term vision? Does it contribute to your overall sense of purpose and fulfillment?

Keep a dedicated notebook or digital document handy where you can jot down your thoughts during each session. This record will be invaluable over time, allowing you to track your evolving motivations and insights. At the end of each session, review your notes to identify any patterns or insights. Then, plan one or two specific actions you can take in the coming month to better align your activities with your "why."

By institutionalizing these Why-FI sessions, you create a powerful ritual that keeps your motivations clear and your actions intentional. This ongoing practice not only reconnects you with your foundational purposes but also empowers you to make informed, deliberate choices about your path forward.

Now, let's unpack these one by one—the three Ps of Personal Pursuit—so we know why they're important.

Progress

When assessing your progress, it's important to recognize and celebrate how far you've come. We become so focused on the challenges ahead that we forget to acknowledge the obstacles we've already overcome. Wherever you're at, take a moment to reflect on the problems you've already solved, the skills you've developed, and the milestones you've achieved since starting your journey. Even the small ones are worth celebrating.

Personally, I struggle with this a lot. I have a tendency to fixate on the road ahead and not give an ounce of celebration to the things I've accomplished. What's next was always more important. I used to categorize this as "driven," but sometimes when you drive too fast, you miss out on all the scenic moments along the way.

Truthfully, I'm still working on this, and it's why these scheduled assessments are so important. For example, when I launched my first podcast in July of 2010, I became obsessed with growing the show, landing big guests, and ranking as high as possible on the charts. When the show didn't take off like I was hoping it would, I almost decided to scrap it because, compared to my blog, it was taking up so much more time for so little return.

Six months later, my bookkeeper told me I had surpassed a total of $1 million in revenue since I had started my business in 2008. I had no idea. This was a wake-up call, as I realized just how much progress I had made and that success doesn't come overnight. So I kept at it with the podcast, and as I now approach my 1,000th episode, I can definitely say it was worth every challenge. Now, I understand the importance of slowing down to appreciate each milestone. It's true what they say. Life is not just about the destination; it's equally about remembering the journey and the lessons learned along the way.

When we don't know what, or who, we're working for, it's hard to know when we've achieved enough and it's time to celebrate. As you evaluate your progress, consider keeping a "win list" or success journal where you regularly record your accomplishments, breakthroughs, and lessons. Celebrating your victories, no matter how small, can provide a powerful source of motivation and self-assurance as you continue along the path.

On the other hand, if you find that you haven't made as much progress as you'd hoped, don't be too hard on yourself. A perceived lack of progress doesn't mean you're doing something wrong or that you're not cut out for this journey. There could be several reasons why progress seems slow or stagnant.

First, consider whether you've given yourself enough time to see meaningful results. Growth happens step by step, and it's easy to overlook the small steps and improvements you're making on a daily basis. To better track and understand these incremental gains, consider breaking your goal down into smaller, manageable milestones. Sustainable progress is a marathon, not a sprint. Patience and persistence are key.

This is something my son recently experienced with his trumpet playing. When he began in the fifth grade, progress was slow and he couldn't hit a high C no matter how hard he tried, which frustrated him. As a trumpet player myself, I promised him that if he kept at it and remained consistent with his practice, it would be one of the easiest notes to hit after that. He didn't believe me but agreed to keep practicing, anyway.

I'll forever remember the day Keoni burst into my office and played a high C in excitement, having just unlocked not just a new note, but a new confidence in his musical journey. This was especially emotional for me because he was playing on the same trumpet I played throughout middle school, high school, college, and drum corps.

It was a proud dad moment, for sure. But it was also more than that. This High C Moment is the inflection point we all need in our learning journeys. Without it, it's hard to keep going. We live for those "High C" Moments. They reveal to us what's possible when we persevere.

At the time of this writing, Keoni is now entering his first year in high school and already participating in marching band activities. He marched with the band during the 4th of July parade, and even asked me—on his own—to take lessons so that he could get even better. Even he knows the value of mentorship to seek growth.

If you've been trying to learn a new skill for a while and still aren't seeing the progress—if you haven't had a "High C" Moment in a while—it might be time to dig a little deeper. Are there skills or knowledge gaps that are holding you back? Are you fully committed to the habits that would facilitate your growth? Are there any obstacles or distractions that are derailing your efforts?

In the next chapter I'll uncover some strategies for exponential and rapid growth, specifically to help you get off any plateaus you've hit, especially if you've been "trying everything, but nothing's working." We'll get there.

Asking these questions isn't about blaming or shaming yourself, but about approaching any new skill with curiosity and a growth mindset. Recognizing there's room for improvement is the first and most crucial step toward making positive change. It takes courage and self-awareness to acknowledge when something isn't working, and this realization can be the catalyst for profound breakthroughs and transformation.

For now, celebrate the fact that you're engaging in this self-reflective work, even if it feels uncomfortable. Every insight and revelation you uncover is bringing you one step closer to your full potential. Growth is not always a straight line but a series of ups, downs, and course corrections that each lead you closer to where you want to be.

Passion

Passion is the fuel that drives us, even in the face of obstacles and setbacks. And if you seem to be in a moment in time when passion for your original inspiration is lacking, it can be easy to lose energy, procrastinate, or more commonly, push toward the new fun thing everyone else is talking about.

When assessing your passion, pay close attention to the activities and aspects of your journey that bring you the most joy, excitement, and fulfillment. These are the elements that are likely most aligned with your natural strengths and interests. This is exactly what helped Paul Jarvis opt out of expanding his web design business and instead focus on personal projects that he felt deeply connected to. His passion was design work and writing, and despite the potential for higher profits in client work, Paul realized he was most passionate about creating content that resonated on a personal level. By homing in on what truly excited him, Paul not only found greater satisfaction in his work but also successfully carved out a unique niche that attracted a dedicated audience. This example shows how aligning your efforts with your passions can not only fulfill you but also differentiate your path to success.

On the flip side, take note of the tasks or responsibilities that consistently drain your energy or feel like chores. While every path has its share of mundane or challenging aspects, a pervasive sense of anxiety or disengagement can be a sign that your passion is waning.

I remember the time when editing my podcast felt like a massive chore, getting to the point that I dreaded recording episodes and scheduling interviews because I knew eventually I'd have to slice and dice the episodes into their final form. In the beginning, it was fun because the idea of having my own show was exciting, but after the honeymoon period it felt like an absolute drag. I lost all the energy I once had for it.

My favorite parts were the conversations I was having, not the editing. In 2011, I almost quit my show altogether. Thankfully, my close friend Chris Ducker talked some sense into me. He has a phrase he likes to repeat—"do what you do best, and delegate the rest"—and it was about time for me to finally listen. So, I hired my first podcast editor, and although there was a learning curve, it was one of the best decisions I've ever made. Today, with thousands of episodes recorded over several different podcasts, I still look forward to the most fun parts of it: connecting with amazing people and unpacking their amazing stories with genuine curiosity.

If you find yourself in a similar slump, don't panic. It's normal for enthusiasm to ebb and flow over time, and there are several strategies you can use to rekindle your spark. Here are some ideas:

- Try infusing more novelty and challenge into your routine, perhaps with a Voluntary Force Function to kick things into high gear that both challenges and lights you up again.

- Connect with others who may be on the same journey as you. There's no better way to get a dose of inspiration or a helpful resource to solve a problem than from others in the community who have traveled the same path you're on. It was through connections I had in the community I was a part of that led to finding my first podcast editor.

- Take a break. Sometimes, you just might need a moment to escape the grind and come back reengaged and reenergized. For some, a walk is all that's needed. For others, it might take longer. My mentor, Michael Hyatt, schedules an entire month out of his year to step away from all work to recharge and come back with even more energy and ideas.

- Be realistic. It's important to remember that passion isn't always a constant state of euphoria or excitement. Sometimes, it's a quieter sense of commitment, purpose, and satisfaction. Don't put pressure on yourself to feel ecstatic all the time. Instead, aim for a steady sense of engagement and fulfillment.

If, after trying these strategies, you still feel a persistent lack of passion, it might be a sign that it's time for a bigger change. This is where the other aspects of self-assessment—alignment, balance, and growth—come into play. A lack of passion can signal a deeper misalignment that needs to be addressed. In these cases, don't be afraid to ask the tough questions: *Is this path still aligned with my values and long-term vision? Am I sacrificing too much in other areas of my life to pursue this goal? Have I outgrown this dream or direction?*

Answering these questions can be challenging, but it's an essential part of the self-assessment process. Trust that your intuition and inner wisdom will guide you along the path that's truly right for you, even if it means making difficult choices or changes.

Remember, a temporary dip in passion doesn't mean you're on the wrong track. It may simply signal that some adjustments or course corrections are needed. That's just part of the process. By staying attuned to your passion and making intentional shifts along the way, you'll ensure your journey remains fulfilling and sustainable for the long haul.

Purpose

When you're in alignment with your purpose, there's a sense of flow and rightness to your endeavors. You feel like you're being true to yourself, even if the path isn't always easy. Your goals and aspirations are in harmony with who you are at your core, and you're able to make decisions and take actions that feel authentic and meaningful.

To paraphrase the work of Mihaly Csikszentmihalyi (try saying that three times fast!), who first brought the idea of flow states to light in his groundbreaking book, *Flow: The Psychology of Optimal Experience*, flow is where challenge meets competency. If we take on a task that is too easy, we become bored. But if we take on something too difficult, we get stressed. But when we attempt something difficult that aligns with our passions and abilities, we start to settle into a state that allows us to fire on all cylinders. We get into flow—and that's where the real magic happens.[1]

Boots Knighton is a member of the SPI Community and has recently experienced the power of purpose in her work. She launched her podcast, *The Heart Chamber Podcast*, in January 2023 to share her story and capture the stories of others who have experienced open heart surgery, too.

She started the show to help patients who are feeling overwhelmed and unsure of what to expect, and when she launched her show, it was a thrill. It was exciting to know she had the ability to help others, but there was just one problem: her show wasn't gaining much traction. She knew, however, that this podcast and sharing her story was her calling. She had gone through those tough times in her life so that she could help and serve others, and she was determined to figure out how to bring more listeners to her show.

Boots showed up to my virtual office hours—where I meet regularly with students and answer any questions they have—

and asked how to get better at marketing her podcast. After getting some help, slowly but surely Boots's numbers began to grow. Soon after surveying her audience and changing the name of her podcast to *Open Heart Surgery with Boots*, she began to experience the exponential growth that was always possible for her. In a celebratory message inside of the SPI Community, she shared, "In just three days, I'm charting in the medicine genre in the US on Apple Podcasts. It's a dream come true!"

As a result of her perseverance and alignment to her passion for this subject, Boots will be able to change the lives of many more people.

Passion becomes determination, as we just saw. But on the flip side, misalignment manifests itself as a nagging sense of unease. In this scenario, you might find yourself frequently second-guessing your decisions, feeling like you're compromising your integrity, or noticing a disconnect between your stated values and your actual behavior.

Other red flags that signal you might be out of alignment include:

- consistently procrastinating or avoiding tasks related to your goals or vision;
- feeling like you're wearing a mask or playing a role that doesn't feel true to who you really are;
- regularly sacrificing your well-being, relationships, or other important priorities for the sake of your work or ambitions;
- experiencing a sense of emptiness or lack of fulfillment, even when you're experiencing success.

If you recognize some of these signs, don't beat yourself up. We all go through periods of misalignment, and recognizing it is the first step to getting back on track.

A Mission Statement for Your ... *Life?*

One powerful exercise for assessing and correcting your alignment is to create your own personal mission statement. This is a clear, concise articulation of your core values, beliefs, and long-term vision for your life and work.

Having this North Star to refer back to can be incredibly clarifying when you're facing tough choices or feeling pulled in different directions, and it can also steer you back in the right direction when you get off course, too. I only wish I had created a personal mission statement sooner, because at one point early in my entrepreneurial journey, not only did I find myself off course, I was beginning to experience the "Dark Side."

Back in 2011, when my architectural business was running virtually on autopilot, I started to experiment with even more ways to generate revenue online. During my research, I came across a story about another blogger who recently hired a developer to create a premium WordPress plugin, and after charging customers $77 to get access to his software, he generated over $100,000 in revenue in less than a week.

At that moment, I mentally morphed into Scrooge McDuck and imagined the giant vault of money I'd be swimming in if I launched my own plugin, too. So I got to work. If you stared hard enough, I bet you could see dollar signs in my eyes, just like in the cartoons.

I immediately hired a developer I found on Google, and we started working together to build a different plugin. The estimated cost was $6,000 and the time frame to complete the project was six weeks. Unfortunately, after six weeks, the plugin wasn't ready yet. We needed more time, and the developer needed more money. After twelve weeks, the plugin still wasn't ready, and like before, we needed more time, and the developer needed even more money. But finally, after six months, the plugin was finished. The total cost: $15,000.

That's a lot more money than I expected, but I kept telling myself that I'd make it all back, and then some. I just had to put it out there and sell it. Here's how it did.

Total revenue: $0.00. I didn't even sell one.

I was so focused on how much money I was going to make, I spent very little time actually thinking about creating a product of real value. Before the launch date, while beta-testing the plugin with a few groups of people, not one person said they would ever pay for it. An anonymous respondent even called it "generic garbage," which definitely stung, but it was true. Even worse, several participants gave me a ton of amazing suggestions on what they actually wanted to see in a plugin. But I was already over budget and had wasted a ton of time.

In the end, I never took the plugin to market.

Although I was out $15,000 and lost six months of my time, it was an expensive lesson that humbled me and gave me exactly what I needed. The sting deflated my ego, and I saw clearly what really mattered when it came to my business—serving first.

From here, I created my first ever mission statement: *To develop and deliver value-first solutions that truly meet my audience's needs, and where community feedback takes priority over profit. My mission is to serve, innovate, and build trust with every product I create.*

Since then, I've been living that mission and have been teaching it to others. It's become a mantra within our community at SPI. If you ever happen to catch me on YouTube, you might even see me sporting a "Serve First" T-shirt. That's how much I believe in this statement; it's almost a mantra to me. And it's just one of my personal mission statements that has helped me stay on track and make better decisions.

To create your own mission statement, ask yourself the following:

1. What are the nonnegotiable principles and values that guide my life and work?
2. What kind of impact do I want to have on the world?
3. What qualities and characteristics do I want to embody in my daily life and interactions?
4. What do success and fulfillment look like for me, beyond external achievements and metrics?

You will definitely need to schedule an additional block of time for this, so when you're ready, place a two-hour block in your calendar for it. (You see, we're doing the things when we need to do the things!)

Take your time with this exercise. Don't censor yourself. The more honest and specific you can be, the more powerful your mission statement will become. It serves as a guidepost for your future and a filter for tough decisions along the way, so don't neglect it.

Once you have a mission statement, use it as a touchstone to evaluate your current path and choices. When faced with a decision or opportunity, ask yourself: *Does this align with my mission and values? Will this move me closer to my long-term vision for my life and work?*

If the answer is no, it might be time to make some adjustments. This could mean saying no to certain commitments, redefining your goals, or even pivoting to a new direction altogether. While change can be scary, remember that realigning with your truth is always worth it in the long run. It's important to remember that alignment is an ongoing process, not a one-time event. As we grow and evolve, our values and visions may shift, too. Make it a regular practice to check in with your mission statement—at least once a quarter—and make sure it still resonates with your current self.

By staying attuned to your alignment and making intentional choices to honor your authenticity, you'll ensure that your journey remains fulfilling and meaningful. Trust that when you're aligned with your deepest truth, the universe will conspire to support you in ways you never could have imagined.

What Next?

If you've read through all of the above and you have yet to schedule your Self-Assessment Session, do that first and then give yourself the time, space, and grace to be honest with yourself as you go through the 3 Ps: Progress, Passion, and Purpose.

If you've already completed the session, you likely have unlocked new excitement and alignment, but also more questions and wonder. This is where the next and last section of this chapter comes into play. Because too often, we can't see what's right in front of us and need an outside perspective to help.

Seeking Feedback from Others

As the saying goes, "You can't read the label when you're inside the bottle." Sometimes, we're so close to our own experiences, thoughts, and behaviors that we can't see ourselves objectively. That's why seeking external feedback is vital to the self-assessment process. Combined with our own self-evaluation, feedback from others can provide valuable insights and perspectives we might not be able to access on our own.

Earlier in the book, we explored the power of finding people in your life who champion your journey. When it comes to soliciting feedback, your personal mentors become a valuable resource. Having walked similar paths themselves, they offer strategic guidance, constructive criticism, and encouragement from a place of experience and wisdom.

But personal mentors aren't the only ones who can provide feedback. If you're part of a mastermind group or other network or community, these can be excellent sources of feedback, as well. These groups unite individuals from diverse backgrounds and industries who can offer fresh perspectives and insights you might not get from your immediate circle.

As you seek feedback, here's a piece of advice from my own learned experience: do not show up and ask for general help. Questions like "What do you think I should work on?" or "Can you help me get better at this?" aren't helpful because it's hard to pinpoint exactly what you might need help with. The more specific you can be, the better.

Here's a question from Amalia, a member of SPI who asked a great, specific question during a recent Ask-Me-Anything in our community. She has a small YouTube channel about yoga:

Hi Pat!
I was wondering what you would recommend for a small YouTube channel that is looking for their first few sponsorships?
I have a wellness channel that is still quite small but it's starting to get a decent following. I'm still too small for companies to think of approaching me so I think I will have to approach them.
Any advice on a good way to do this?
Also, a pricing structure that is fair for a small channel?

As a guide inside of SPI, I can easily tap into my own specific experiences and resources to help Amalia much more easily with a question like this. Getting specific, however, is not always easy. If you need help to get more specific with your asks, use what you've learned in your self-assessment as a starting point. Be open and receptive to the feedback you receive, even (and especially) if it's not what you expected or hoped to hear. Thank the network responders for their insights and consider how you can implement their suggestions.

In addition to professional contexts, seeking feedback from friends and family can be valuable as well, especially when it comes to personal growth and development. These are the people who know you best and want to see you happy, healthy, and fulfilled. When approaching friends or family, choose individuals you trust to be honest, compassionate, and supportive. Avoid those who tend to be overly judgmental, as their feedback may not be helpful.

Personally, I had a certain set of "friends" from my architecture days who were definitely not supportive of my decision to become an entrepreneur. They'd joke with me that one day I'd be back at a "real job," and during the occasional lunch or coffee meetup, it always felt like they were belittling me for "ditching my degree" and wasting my career away. It was hard to hear. But as soon as I began publishing my business journey online and sharing my successes, those lunch invitations dried up. Turns out, it's tough to eat when you're eating your words.

At the same time, if you have a hype crew who, no matter what you do, always tell you how awesome you are, it's crucial to balance that with more grounded feedback. While cheerleading can boost your morale, it might not always provide the constructive criticism needed to foster real growth. It's great to feel supported, but make sure you also have people who can challenge you and keep you accountable—those who aren't afraid to tell it like it is when you need to hear it.

Of course, soliciting external feedback can make you feel vulnerable and uncomfortable. But when approached with curiosity, humility, and a genuine desire to grow, it can be one of the most transformative practices we engage in. Growth only happens when we're challenged. This whole process, in a way, is a Voluntary Force Function. As you gather feedback from mentors, peers, friends, and family, look for common themes or patterns that emerge. What insights or suggestions come up again and again? These are the areas that warrant the most attention.

At the same time, remember that feedback is just that. It's data, not destiny. *You* get to decide what to do with the insights you receive and how to integrate them into your growth. The most successful people in the world are the ones constantly seeking out new ways to learn, grow, and improve. By embracing feedback as a tool for self-discovery and transformation, you'll be well on your way to joining their ranks.

This journey of Lean Learning is never a straight line. But through continuous self-reflection and timely pivots, we can ensure that every step aligns with a bigger vision for our lives. As Eric Ries, author of *The Lean Startup*, puts it: "A pivot is a change in strategy without a change in vision."

Looking ahead to the next chapter, we're set to explore new heights in our endeavors. Think of it like leveling up in a video game. You've accumulated enough experience points—now it's time to harness those new skills and amplify your impact. Let's go!

7.

Micro Mastery and Quantum Leaps

"Fortune favors the bold."

—Latin Proverb

At some point in our journey, we encounter pivotal moments that demand we either evolve or stay stagnant. Whether through the process of taking tiny, deliberate steps—what I call "Micro Mastery"—or embarking on more significant, audacious moves—"Quantum Leaps"—the path to personal and professional transformation is rarely straightforward.

This chapter will explore both approaches: how to cultivate painstaking precision in your efforts and when to make big, bold moves.

Let's get into it.

Ori Bengal was a world traveler and blogger. But I, like many others, knew him as "Couch Surfing Ori." As a self-proclaimed professional couch surfer, Ori blogged about his crazy adventures, finding ways to temporarily stay at people's houses and apartments while hopscotching across the United States.

From college campuses to the guest rooms of multimillionaires, Ori saw it all. Along with his many followers and fans, I was living vicariously through his adventures. But I was also inspired by the stories he told about the different people and families he befriended in the process, as well as the influence he gained from meeting them.

In 2010, I actually had the pleasure of meeting Couch Surfing Ori at an event. He made money through various internet marketing efforts—just enough to scrape by, but still, a living!—including building websites for people. Which is why he was there at that marketing conference.

I can't remember whose couch he was sleeping on that night, but I do remember his infectious personality, and I admired his go-with-the-flow attitude. Deep down, though, underneath his adventurous spirit, Ori harbored a quiet void, a secret I would soon discover. In spite of being a successful world traveler and digital entrepreneur, Ori had abandoned his passion for art.

As someone who had grown up loving drawing and painting and sculpture, Ori had come a long way from his roots. But after a failed art show as a young adult where not a single person purchased any of his pieces, Ori put away the paintbrushes.

For years, he would label himself as an "internet marketer who had failed at art," a label that only reinforced his sense of personal defeat. But in 2012, after a decade of not sketching a single line, Ori was couch surfing in Hawaii when he was invited by a friend to an art gallery.

Reluctantly, he went.

And there, standing amid the inspiring works of art, Ori felt both heartache and hope as he realized how he had abandoned his true passion and first love. In that moment, he decided to reconnect with art once again. It was time to create.

Ori started implementing a simple strategy to improve his then somewhat rusty creative skills and stay the course as an artist, despite whatever discouragements he might encounter. Soon after his trip to Hawaii, he posted an announcement on Facebook that he was going to create a new piece of art every day.

This was a simple way to provide just enough public pressure to hold Ori accountable, knowing that consistency would help him improve much faster than anything else. He also received a lot of support from his followers, who had the opportunity to help him name his pieces as he created them each day. It was a communal effort.

Ori also embraced the power of imperfection. Art is subjective, so it's not right to say what's *good* and what's not, but even *he* would share what he didn't like about his pieces and how he was intending to improve next time. The artist-in-training wisely embraced progress, not perfection—as we all must.

The most fascinating and unique observation about Ori, though, was that over the course of posting more than 4,000 daily art pieces, you can see a timeline of deliberate attempts to improve on just one small detail at a time. It's fascinating to look at his work in aggregate. Thanks to the layout of social media photo albums, you can see Ori's evolution gradually unfolding in each piece he has posted over the years, almost like you're able to travel back in time and understand what skill he was trying to get better at and when.

In a recent conversation, he shared with me, "In order to improve, I'd have to go very small with my focus, like extremely small. You start general, then figure out what the subcomponents are . . . then figure out which ones are most important. That's what you focus on, and even then, you can break it down even more."

Today, not only have Ori's art skills improved dramatically since he restarted, but his art is now being commissioned by people from all around the world, including celebrities like David Copperfield and William Shatner. He even partnered with rock star Alice Cooper to raise $10,000 for charity with one of his pieces.

Ori's story may seem like a tale of finding renewed inspiration, and it definitely is, but it's also an inspiring case of Lean Learning. And it teaches us a valuable lesson. Inspiration alone wasn't enough to help Ori succeed, nor did any of his success happen overnight. Rather, his achievements required a series of small, incremental improvements that, over time, grew to yield incredible results. This is what mastery truly looks like: a million small attempts that add up over time.

Improving One Small Skill at a Time

Lean Learners don't just take random action but focus on the smaller components required in learning any skill. This is Micro Mastery, which involves paying attention to small, specific, incremental changes that compound over time to create significant results. These changes are about identifying specific elements within a repeated behavior or skill to achieve targeted improvements—they go hand in hand with habits.

A person, for example, may develop a habit of running thirty minutes a day. But by applying Micro Mastery, they can dedicate a single week to perfecting their running posture, followed by another week of concentrating on breathing techniques to enhance their lung capacity. And so on.

This compartmentalized and focused approach to personal development allows for quicker, more effective improvements across all aspects of a skill. It also allows us to mimic the same kind of learning environments that a coach would guide us through, temporarily hyperfocusing on one part of a much larger whole. It takes habits to a whole new level.

When I was in high school and in college, I played in the band. This is no surprise to anyone who knows my nerdy tendencies, but this was the first real environment where I understood how difficult it was to get really good at something. It was not enough to just put in the hours and memorize your music. To become a great performer, we had to do more.

When we were practicing, the conductor didn't just have us play the same old songs from start to finish over and over again. He siloed the more difficult parts and had us repeat those parts with continual improvements each time. If we got it wrong, he'd stop, shake his head, and tell us to start over. Sometimes, we'd break it down even further by instrument, and sometimes even further by individual players.

It was embarrassing when you were the reason he stopped the whole band, but this practice taught us when our personal definition of "good enough" was nowhere near good enough. Over time, we learned to take pride in the music we were eventually able to make, because we knew how hard we'd practiced and how much work it had taken to get a piece ready to perform. To level up our musical skills, we had to break things down again and again, almost painstakingly so—and I never forgot that.

When I took golf lessons (inspired by my coworker George), I wasn't taught to swing off the tee with a driver, hit an approach shot with an iron, putt from long distances, or rescue myself from a sand trap all in one day. Instead, the coach and I focused on one element of the game at a time, like putting.

But even that wasn't small enough. There were, in fact, entire hour-long sessions specifically focused on how to read the slopes of the greens, how to make contact with the ball when you were putting, and more. It was meticulous work, rarely exciting, and sometimes downright frustrating. But you know what? I got pretty good. Not as good as George, of course, but definitely better than Terry. *Sorry, Terry (not sorry).*

This is Micro Mastery in action—taking tiny steps toward improvement that all add up to something great.

In Ori's case, it would have been rare for a fan to scroll through his Facebook and see him publishing random things. That wasn't what he was doing. Instead, you'd see large chunks of time when he was making self-portraits, evidenced by a lot of images of his face in different styles. Scroll a little further, and you'd find sci-fi-inspired art with otherworldly creatures and creations. Lots and lots of it, with little tweaks, all adding up to longer-term improvements in his form and style. Other times, the common denominator was a specific color or a different perspective.

In each snapshot of Ori's timeline, you could see him hyperfocused on improving one thing until he figured it out and was satisfied with the results. Then, he would move on to the next micro skill he wanted to master. Later, he told me that he got so exacting with his focus that sometimes he fixated on just how to use different brushes. This is what every master knows that the rest of us don't: we can only get good at one thing at a time. True mastery is the cultivation of many skills, each honed individually.

Using Micro Mastery

Recently, I was asked to deliver the closing keynote at Social Media Marketing World, a marketing event that happens each year in my backyard of San Diego. Well, not my literal backyard, because backyards don't really exist in California, but we do have nice weather.

Anyway . . .

Although I've spoken at hundreds of events around the world now and have gotten pretty good at delivering a keynote, I'm always looking for ways to acquire new skill points and level up my game. So, as I do with every talk, I decided I was going to hyperfocus on one aspect of speaking I had not gone deep with yet. And in this case, that was using metaphors.

Metaphors are a powerful teaching tool used to clarify concepts quickly and make ideas stick, and I knew if I could nail one for this talk, it would drive home my point even better. The topic I was asked to speak on was long-form video content and why I favored it over short-form platforms like TikTok and Instagram Reels.

I don't hate short-form content, but in my view, long-form wins, hands down, every time. There's just no comparison to the depth you can take your audience with it, as well as the long-term relationship you can build with others, and the higher ad revenues. Still, at an event where six other well-known speakers were giving talks on the power of short-form content in their businesses, I knew that I needed a really powerful message to make my case.

So I decided a metaphor was the way to go:

Short-form content is like handing out candy on Halloween. Sure, you might get a lot of people coming over to get something sweet, but what happens after that? They move on to the next house, and then the next one, and the next after that. Online, your short-form video is one house on a road of endless "doom scrolling," and within seconds, you're forgotten.

Personally, I'd rather be the chef at a restaurant serving a three-course meal, one where my audience can sit down, savor the dishes, and enjoy conversation with their company. They don't just remember the experience, but talk about it to others when they get home, even the next day. They want to come back and try other dishes next time. And although it's harder to cook a meal like this, as opposed to buying a bag of candy and handing it out, it's worth it.

Creating content like this is how you build loyal fans for life.

I practiced multiple styles of how to deliver this metaphor to the audience. I tried different slides to support the story, even thought about a live demo with candy onstage or finding a chef's hat. Before the event, I micro-tested this metaphor live during my office hours in the SPI Community to gauge audience reactions and make sure it made sense to others.

The talk landed. Not only did I get my point across, but several people, including sponsors at the event, came up to me afterward to specifically reference that metaphor. One woman even said, "I'm so tired of handing out Halloween candy, thank you!"

Micro Mastery is a useful and necessary practice that I try to implement in everything I do. While podcasting, I focus on asking better follow-up questions. While working out, I pay attention to my posture during rows so that I don't strain my lower back. While swimming, I watch the entry of my hands into the water. And while playing Fortnite with my kids, I try to improve my reaction time and aim using an aim trainer called KovaaK's.

Not all micro improvements significantly change the quality of the output. But over time, the results start to compound, and depending on how it's applied, it can more quickly get you to that Victory Royale (that's what they call a win in Fortnite for you noobs).

The Compounding Effects of Micro Skill Development

In my business, the most significant type of Micro Mastery my team and I practice is focusing on specific components of our sales funnels. By focusing our team's shared brainpower on improving each part in the process, this improves our results in astounding, and often surprising, ways. For instance, take a look at the basic funnel below (I'm using a 10 percent conversion rate for easy math).

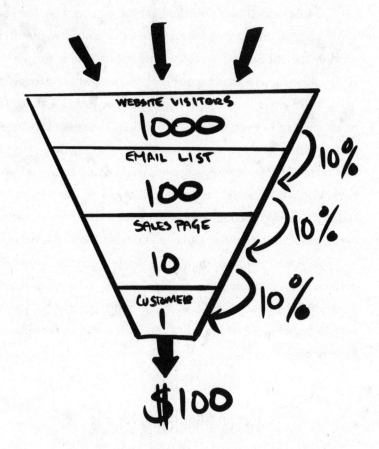

Let's say it's our first week of business, and we have a website that sells a $100 product (this is all hypothetical to illustrate a point). When 1,000 visitors go to our website, 10 percent of those people will join our email list, which means there're 100 people on the list. Out of those 100 people on the list, 10 percent click a link to view the sales page, which means 10 people look at it. Out of those 10 people, 10 percent of *them* convert to a sale, which means one person purchased the product.

So we earned $100.

Simple math, right? But here's where it gets interesting: imagine now that you apply Micro Mastery to improve your email-to-sales-page conversions.

Doing this, we can use Just-in-Time Information to help us find an expert with up-to-date marketing strategies that we can implement and test. We will also give ourselves one week to implement those changes so that we can see the results and iterate accordingly.

In Week 2, another 1,000 people visit the website. One hundred of them (10 percent) join the email list. But because we applied Micro Mastery and focused our efforts on email-list-to-sales-page conversions, our conversion rate is now 20 percent instead of 10 percent. This means that 20 people will now visit the sales page, and at a 10 percent conversion rate, that's two purchases instead of one.

We just made $200.

By doubling the conversion rate, we doubled the sales. Not bad, right? We didn't even have to add any more traffic, which is what most people think about doing first. Again, this is all still fairly simple. But remember that Micro Mastery is about stacking incremental changes on top of each other, then seeing the exponential increase over time. You're starting to see the compounding effects of focusing on one piece of a complex process at a time, hyperfocusing on improving that piece, then seeing the results of your effort. But we're just getting started.

Let's keep going.

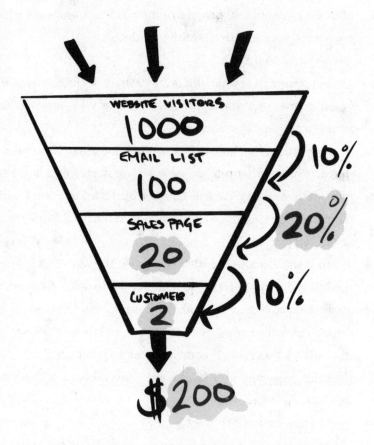

Since we've got some quick wins on the email-list-to-sales-page conversions, let's now apply Micro Mastery to our website-visitors-to-email-list conversion rate. As before, we find Just-in-Time Information to help us hyperfocus on this particular detail of the funnel.

For a day, we focus just on subject lines so that we can increase the open rates of our emails. Then, for another day, it's all about increasing deliverability (i.e., the number of emails that end up in a person's inbox versus their spam folder). And then another day, we focus on creating a compelling offer, like a free guide to download if a person subscribes to the list.

During Week 3, another 1,000 visit our website. However, this time (thanks to our Micro Mastery efforts), 30 percent of people convert, which means 300 people now enter the email list.

From there, since we also improved our email-to-sales-page conversion rates in Week 2, 20 percent of those 300 people view our sales page, which is a total of 60 people. At the same conversion rate as before, we made six sales for a total of $600. And that's with the same number of people visiting the website. We've now tripled our results within a week.

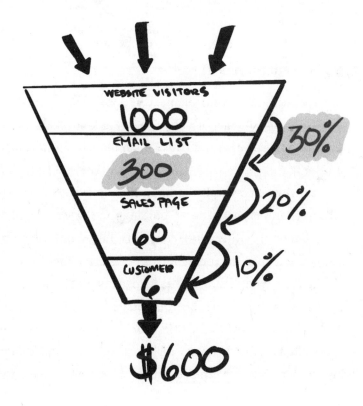

As you can see, the numbers start to grow quickly when you focus on one piece at a time—and you could clearly keep going, continually improving each piece of the funnel over and over again, maximizing conversions, increasing website visitors, and getting more "squeeze" out of your lemon, so to speak.

The power of Micro Mastery lies in its accessibility and sustainability. By focusing on small, incremental changes, you make the process of growth more manageable and less overwhelming. This approach in our learning journey helps us maintain motivation and momentum, allowing each of us to see tangible progress along the way, even if the ultimate goal seems far off. Little steps, over time and with continual improvement, can create massive results.

Getting Micro: How It Works

Incorporating this kind of mastery into your learning journey is a game-changer. It's like mastering knife skills as a chef. Everything revolves around this fundamental skill; and once you master it, you can move on and stack another skill on top of it.

It's why when you listen to an interview with Jimmy Donaldson (aka MrBeast), the #1 YouTuber in the world with over 300 million subscribers, he'll constantly talk about what he's hyperfocusing on at the moment to grow his channel.

In 2019, when I saw MrBeast speak at VidSummit, his entire talk was about YouTube thumbnails—the images that show up on YouTube next to the title. More recently, he's been public about the fact that he's focusing on storytelling and building a deeper connection to the characters in his challenges. This is what, in part, helps him make a video that gets seen by millions of people around the world within minutes of publishing it.

Don't ever let someone tell you, "Don't sweat the small stuff." Because it's all small stuff! And sometimes, paying close attention to those little details can pay off big-time. Of course, we first have to get a big picture of what we want to do and where we want to go—which is where your "why" comes in. But to get truly great at anything requires strict attention and focus.

By identifying specific areas for improvement, committing to consistent effort, and embracing the cumulative impact of small changes, you can unlock significant growth and progress in any area of life. Micro Mastery is, effectively, Lean Learning *within* Lean Learning.

As you consider what to apply this practice to, here are some actionable steps to take:

1. **Break it down . . . then break it down some more.** With the skill, behavior, or goal you want to improve, break it down into smaller micro skills, as small as you can get for the skills you need to meet your goals.

2. **Prioritize the parts.** Once you've finished the breakdown into smaller pieces, put them in order of which actions you'd like to take. Which one will you start with? What will you try after that? Consider what skills may offer the most benefit and which ones might be easiest to implement sooner rather than later. Make a decision, and choose one.

3. **Set clear goals.** Establish clear, measurable goals for the next micro improvement you want to make. This will help you track your progress and stay motivated. Be sure to make a clear decision for how long you're going to focus on this micro skill.

4. **Collect Just-in-Time Information.** Before you begin taking action, find the resources needed to learn the best way to maximize your results. Whether it's from champions who have had more experience before you or the newest resources available, find what you need, and get ready to apply it.

5. **Go!** With your new information in hand, execute on this micro skill. With every iteration comes potential improvement, and reps are important. Give it a shot, do your best, and keep going.

6. **Be patient.** Remember that Micro Mastery is a long-term approach. It takes time and consistent effort to see real results, so go easy on yourself and trust the process. Couch Surfing Ori did not see results right away—but over time, his skills stacked in significant ways, and he improved exponentially on his creative output.

7. **Celebrate your wins.** Acknowledge and celebrate each micro improvement you make, no matter how small. It's one step toward a bigger goal, and you

need to stay motivated and encouraged. This will help you remain positive, even if progress feels slow.

8. **Select the next skill.** Then repeat the process all over again. The more you do this to as many pieces of a process as you can, the greater impact you will have.

Whether you're working on a specific skill, habit, or goal, breaking it down into the smallest, most manageable components and focusing on consistent improvements will help you unlock your full potential and achieve the success you want.

Quantum Leaps

Incremental improvements stack over time and eventually lead to life-changing results, but there's also another way to accelerate your growth trajectory: by taking Quantum Leaps.

The concept of a "quantum leap" comes, of course, from quantum mechanics. It describes an electron's sudden transition from one energy level to another. A Quantum Leap in personal or professional growth, however, involves making a sudden and substantial shift that catapults your progress and transforms your achievements in a remarkably short period of time.

While Micro Mastery focuses on steady, methodical progress, Quantum Leaps are about seizing those pivotal moments that promise significant rewards and embracing the bold changes necessary to achieve them. It's about taking calculated risks and pushing beyond what you're comfortable with. Because as Regina King once said, "The comfort zone is where your dreams come to die."

There are two types of Quantum Leaps we can take—one requires a mostly permanent decision, and another a mostly temporary one. Both, however, require you to be brave and willing to leave the familiar behind.

Let's look, for example, at how my friend Nathan Barry exemplified this when he faced a crucial decision point in his career.

Shut Down, Or Double Down?

In 2012, Nathan Barry was a successful designer and author who had generated over half a million dollars in online sales with his digital products. He wanted to scale up and earn even more, but he came across a major roadblock—the email tools he was using were just not optimized for the kind of sales he was doing.

So, Nathan designed and built a tool that would work better, and eventually called it ConvertKit. A tool he had originally designed to solve his own problem, he thought, could be something other creators like himself could benefit from. It was a brand-new tool that set out to shake up the online marketing industry.

But despite Nathan's success, ConvertKit struggled to gain any real traction.

Two years into the venture, the company was making between $1,200 and $1,300 per month, and customers were starting to cancel their plans. The online marketing landscape was at the time (and still is) quite competitive. But Nathan knew every other service fell short on the exact features bloggers like him needed to run an online business. Faced with this plateau, he knew he had to make an important call: *Keep going, or shut the thing down entirely.*

On the one hand, Nathan really believed in ConvertKit and what he was building. But on the other hand, his self-publishing business continued to generate substantial revenue every year. He felt conflicted.

One evening after dinner—while attending a conference—Nathan had a life-altering conversation with his friend Hiten Shah, the founder of KISSmetrics and Crazy Egg. Hiten confirmed Nathan's doubts.

"You know, Nathan," he said, "you should just shut down ConvertKit."

Hiten was an experienced founder and developer who knew the company was eventually going to die in its current state.

"You're almost two years into ConvertKit at this point. It doesn't have traction. It's shrinking. You should shut it down."

Then, Hiten stopped in the middle of the sidewalk, and Nathan did the same.

"*Or . . .* you can take it seriously," Hiten said. "You can give it the time, money, and attention it deserves and build it into a *real* company. You've got a bunch of these other things going on, and you're split between a lot of it. Shut it down, or double down."

The advice resonated with Nathan. As the saying goes: "What got you here won't get you there." Making the decision to double down on ConvertKit was a bold move for Nathan, and a brave one, fraught with risks and unknowns. It would require him to step away from his successful publishing venture and dedicate himself fully to turning his small start-up around, all with a wife and two young kids at home. There was no guarantee of success. The only thing he was sure of was that continuing to straddle both businesses was not a viable long-term strategy.

When Nathan asked himself, "Have I given this every possible chance to succeed?" the honest answer was *no*. After some time and a lot of calculated risk and follow-up conversations, he chose to embrace uncertainty and look to the possibility of what this big decision could open up for him, his family, and the world.

In other words, Nathan doubled down. He shut down the self-publishing business (despite it easily making six figures per year), and went all in on ConvertKit, taking $50,000 out of his retirement savings to fund the project. He invested all of his time, money, and resources into scaling this company and competing with the big brands that had been owning the space for years.

I personally connected with Nathan in 2014 when he asked me to join his advisory board, so I've had a unique perspective on this transformation. It's been a wild ride and fun to have a front-row seat to all these decisions.

By the end of 2015, now fully focused on ConvertKit, Nathan Barry was able to take his dying company from $1,200 in revenue per month to over $98,000 per month. Today, the company (now rebranded "Kit") has grown to a team of seventy-four members across forty-nine cities in North America, Europe, Asia, and New Zealand. It has literally become a household name in the world of email marketing, generating over $100,000 per day (yes, per day).

The lesson? With bold decisions come potentially big results. Nathan placed his bet, and with his full attention pushed all his chips to the center of the table, and played the best hand he could. And it paid off.

What could doubling down on a big dream make possible for *you*?

The Principle of a Power 10

While Quantum Leaps demand big, bold, and brave actions, they do not always have to be all-or-nothing. Many of my students on the brink of success don't need to change their business models. They may just need to change their area of focus for a brief moment in time, so that they can get a bigger picture of what's possible. Chances are, you're in a similar position. If you're like a lot of people I know, you've got a lot on your plate, you're focused on too many things all at once, and you're not seeing the results you want.

This is how you know it's time to insert a "Power 10."

In 2002, during my sophomore year at UC Berkeley, my roommates convinced me to join the Cal rowing team, also known simply as crew.

Cal has always had a prestigious and competitive rowing program, up there with the likes of Harvard, Princeton, Washington, and Yale. But just to set the record straight, I joined the lightweight crew, not the heavyweight crew, which actually included several members with Olympic experience. I swear, they were like real-life Vikings. (And I was just a junior Viking, like the scrawny guy in *How to Train Your Dragon*.)

Anyway, I joined the rowing team to meet new friends and get in a good workout, but over time, rowing became my life. At 5 a.m. every weekday morning, I found myself rowing through the San Francisco Bay with my fellow crewmates, watching the sun rise and reflect on the glassy water our oars were breaking through in a synchronous and hypnotic motion. It was beautiful.

At the same time, it was absolute torture. Rowing in college is one of the hardest things I have ever put myself through. The daily workouts pushed my body to the limit, and it wasn't uncommon for us, especially on test days, to throw up after a workout right into the Bay (how's that for an image?).

But for some reason, we still kept coming back for more.

On race days, with adrenaline pumping through our bodies and Golden Bear pride on the line, it was as much a mental game as a physical one. In a race, you're already moving incredibly fast, but when the other boat starts pulling ahead, you might need some extra fuel to move even faster.

That's where the Power 10 comes in.

It's up to the coxswain, the person yelling commands to the rowers in the boat, to initiate it. When he or she feels the time is right, in the middle of the race, they'll prepare the rowers by saying:

"All right here it comes, a Power 10 in . . . 3 . . . (stroke) . . . 2 . . . (stroke) . . . 1 . . . (stroke) . . . GO!"

That's the cue for you and every other rower in the boat to go *all out* during the next ten consecutive strokes. The strokes per minute remain the same, but the power behind each stroke increases exponentially. They are ten powerful strokes to move you ahead of the competition.

If you happen to be watching from the shore, you'll immediately see a boat performing a Power 10 cut through the water like a hot knife hitting butter. It's incredible to watch.

But if you happen to be *inside* the boat during a Power 10, it's like you're flying. You literally feel the momentum shift in a moment after that first stroke, and even though you're in pain and don't believe you have any more to give, you somehow find more to give.

It's just ten strokes, after all, and that's why it works so well. Everyone can always find the strength for another ten strokes. That's the idea of a Power 10—it's a contained moment of heightened energy that gets you to the next level and ahead of the boats beside you.

It's not unlike a Voluntary Force Function in that it's meant to pull greatness out of you that you aren't sure is possible. Power 10s, in our learning journeys, are intense, short bursts of effort meant to create immediate, significant impact. They're used to overcome short-term hurdles or make quick progress in a competitive situation. The impact is always visible and immediate, providing a burst of results that can shift the momentum in almost any project. It's not about sustainable growth but about seizing a brief opportunity or overcoming an otherwise insurmountable obstacle.

Imagine, for example, that you're working out at the gym by yourself with a goal to improve your fitness. A Voluntary Force Function would be signing up for a fitness class that meets three times a week. It's a commitment that structures your routine and pushes you past your comfort zone on a regular basis. You can't easily back out, because you've already committed to the schedule, the instructor, and perhaps even to a penalty for missed classes. This force function strategically embeds itself into your lifestyle, requiring a consistent, dedicated effort that gradually builds strength and endurance.

On the other hand, a Power 10 is like sprinting the final minute of your thirty-minute treadmill run. It's a short, intense burst that tests your limits and accelerates your performance, but it's fleeting. This sharp, focused effort is not about sustained change but about proving to yourself what you're capable of achieving in a high-energy, condensed period. It's thrilling, challenging, and immensely satisfying, but it's a momentary push rather than a long-term strategy.

That's the difference.

Both strategies have their place in driving progress, but they serve different purposes and are effective in different scenarios. A Voluntary Force Function sets up a systematic approach to growth, while a Power 10 provides an immediate, intense boost to surpass immediate barriers.

And now, back to rowing...

You can run a Power 10 anytime during a race, but the more you use it, the more tired your team will get. Every boat has to manage both the physical strength and mental toughness of their rowers, and when you push too hard for too long, you tire everyone out. On the flip side, if you don't push hard enough, you'll lose. The same is true with learning and skill acquisition. Sometimes, we have to muster extra energy and motivation to reach our next inflection point, but we have to choose when and how best to sprint to get our best results. And, of course, just like with rowing, if all we do is apply nice-and-easy effort, we will never reach our potential. Learning to use Power 10s is an art that takes practice.

Power 10s in Practice

All of us eventually fall into a certain rhythm of life, like another stroke in our boat that keeps us moving forward. You know: *merrily, merrily, merrily*—and all that. But our goals and ambitions don't have to be "but a dream" (sorry, corny reference). They can become a reality, and a Power 10 is a great strategy to get there.

A short burst of effort can dramatically accelerate a person's progress. This principle is particularly effective when you feel stuck or when you're close to a breakthrough but feel unable to make the final push. This move is about concentrating your energy and resources on a few critical tasks that will yield the most significant results.

Again, you have to be careful and calculated with a Power 10; however, when properly leveraged, it's incredibly powerful.

In the world of coding, for example, we might call this a "hackathon"—a period of usually twenty-four to forty-eight hours when coders compete to develop new software solutions from scratch. Participants dive deep into intense collaborative efforts, pushing through the night to innovate, debug, and demonstrate a functioning project by the end of the event. This sort of sprint leads to breakthroughs in technology, the birth of start-up ideas, even to discovering future collaborators and co-founders.

Hackathons harness the energy of a Power 10 by pushing teams to maximize creativity and productivity in a compressed time frame, showcasing what can be achieved when focus and effort are at their peak. It's a way to put yourself into a flow state so that you can get the seemingly impossible done in less time than you anticipated.

Similarly, authors engage in Power 10s in the form of writing retreats. During these retreats, a writer may seclude themselves in a cabin or at a countryside getaway for a few weeks, sometimes more, dedicating most of their free time and energy to finishing their manuscript. This period of uninterrupted focus allows the author space to dive deep into their book and produce significant output, maybe even achieving unprecedented creative feats.

Legend has it that Jack Kerouac famously wrote *On the Road* over the course of a weekend. Of course, there may have been a fair amount of illegal substances involved in the process, but his results were undeniable. So, you know. Maybe don't copy everything Jack did. Nonetheless, the point is that human beings can do incredible things in short amounts of time when they want to get the work done.

For example, the book you're currently reading was finished with a Power 10. Heading off to a remote cabin for months on end wasn't in the cards for me. I couldn't just leave behind my family and responsibilities for that long, nor were any mind-altering substances involved (other than copious amounts of coffee). But I still found a way to dial in my focus and make substantial progress.

Here's how: instead of nibbling at the manuscript bit by bit every day, which I had already done for months with little progress, I carved out two solid weeks where my book was the top priority in my life. During this time, I put other projects on hold and made sure my family understood why I couldn't join them for those fun days at the pool. I woke up early on those days, starting my writing before anyone else in the house was awake, so that I could fully focus on the task at hand.

It was a short-term sacrifice for a significant leap forward, and it worked. This intense and focused approach to the project helped me get through my first major revision way faster than if I had tried to fit writing into the nooks and crannies of daily life. The same could be true for you and whatever current challenge you just can't seem to overcome.

My wife and I even use the principle of Power 10s at home. Every summer before school starts, my wife leads a "purge week" where everyone in the family, including the kids, is in charge of removing and organizing clothes and items we don't use anymore. Everything removed gets donated, and the house can be clean as we start a fresh school year. The kids and I are pretty crummy at consistently maintaining a clean house, so my wife has learned that when we hyperfocus our efforts in bursts like this, we're able to make so much more progress. She's a smart woman.

Whatever the situation, a Power 10 helps you accelerate progress in any project. Knowing there's an end to the sprint helps you push harder than you would otherwise. I encourage you to find ways to incorporate this same tool into your own learning.

How to Implement a Power 10

To leverage this power of focused effort, first identify a single area in your business or personal goals where you need a quick, impactful boost. Maybe it's a project that's been lingering for too long or a skill you need to enhance swiftly to meet an upcoming deadline. Once you've pinpointed these areas, plan your own Power 10 using the POWER structure below:

1. **(P)lan your goals:** Just as a coxswain decides when to call for a Power 10 during a race, determine what you specifically want to achieve during this intense period. This could involve finishing a project, reaching out to potential clients, or mastering a new tool that enhances your productivity.

2. **(O)rganize time and resources:** Prepare by setting a strict, predefined time limit for your intense effort—like ten days of intensive work or ten hours spread over a few days—and gathering all necessary tools and information. This step should include blocking out your calendar, turning off notifications, and/or arranging for external help or collaboration if needed.

3. **(W)ork intensely:** Execute with intensity during your Power 10, focusing deeply on the task or tasks at hand. It's not about extending your hours but

about intensifying your focus and output during the time allocated. Imagine each task as a stroke in the water, where every effort you make brings you closer to your goal.

4. **(E)valuate your progress:** Monitor your progress in real time, adjusting your tactics as needed to stay on track toward your objectives. This step is crucial for maintaining momentum and ensuring that each effort is as effective as possible.

5. **(R)ecover and reflect:** After your Power 10, take time to cool down and review your results, just as rowers do after a race. Reflect on what worked, what didn't, and how you can improve for next time. This recovery phase is essential for learning from the experience and planning your next steps.

Incorporating Power 10s into your routine can transform the way you work and live. It's not about constantly working at a high intensity, which can lead to burnout, but about knowing when to inject a burst of energy to propel you forward. This technique helps you overcome plateaus and achieve significant milestones, making the journey toward your goals not just successful, but exhilarating.

The Bold and the Beautiful (Er, I mean "the Brave")

Making a bold move is not about taking blind leaps of faith or reckless risks. It's about carefully assessing your current situation, identifying opportunities for transformative change, and having the courage to pursue them—even in the face of uncertainty and discomfort.

Now, you might be thinking, "But my goals aren't that grand or world-changing, Pat. I'm just trying to learn a new skill or improve at my craft, not invent the flux capacitor." That's okay. Not everyone's journey requires the same level of boldness and bravery as starting a multimillion-dollar company or leading a social movement (or going back in time for that matter, but I digress). Even in pursuit of seemingly smaller skills or personal goals, there are still moments when a bold move will make all the difference.

If you're wanting to learn how to sing, for example, you could sign up for an open mic night even if it terrifies you. Or, say, you're an aspiring video editor who's been honing your skills on small projects. The bold move might be to reach out to a big-name YouTuber or brand and offer your services, even if you feel like you're not quite ready.

That's exactly what David Rock, an aspiring videographer out of New York City, did in 2014 when he asked best-selling author and entrepreneur Gary Vaynerchuk if he could be his daily cameraman. DRock (as he came to be known) and Gary ended up working together for over nine years! It was an audacious request, and it paid off. A bold move doesn't have to be some grandiose, life-altering decision. It can be any action that pushes you beyond your current limitations, challenges you to grow in new ways, and opens up new opportunities for learning and impact.

Cultivating the habit of making these bold moves, even on a small scale, is essential for anyone who wants to achieve mastery and fulfillment in their life and work. Because the truth is that growth and comfort rarely coexist. If you want to keep progressing and reaching new levels of skill and impact, you have to be willing to step outside your comfort zone and take on new challenges.

So as you reflect on your own inspirational journey, ask yourself:

1. Where might a bold move take me?
2. What opportunities for growth and impact am I leaving on the table by playing it safe?
3. What small, courageous action could I take today to push myself beyond my current limitations?

Being brave doesn't mean being reckless or fearless. It means having the courage to act in the face of what you don't know and may be afraid of. It means trusting in your ability to handle whatever challenges and opportunities arise, and staying committed to your vision even when the path is unclear. Whether your next big move is as simple as raising your hand in class or as grand as a plan to colonize Mars, the principles and strategies in this chapter can help you navigate the process with clarity, confidence, and resilience.

Ultimately, making a bold move requires taking action and embracing the journey ahead. This means letting go of perfectionism, embracing failure as a learning opportunity, and trusting in your ability to adapt and grow along the way. But most of all, making a bold move requires courage—the courage to let go of the familiar, to trust your vision and abilities, and to take action in the face of fear and doubt.

As you contemplate your next bold move, remember that the journey ahead may be challenging, but it is also filled with opportunities for growth, learning, and impact. By staying true to your values, staying open to new possibilities, and embracing the journey with resilience and adaptability, you can achieve extraordinary results and create a life of purpose and fulfillment. So take a deep breath, trust yourself, and take that next brave step. The world is waiting for you to make your mark.

8.

From Learning to Leading

"While we teach, we learn."

—Seneca

When I was still at my architecture job, I remember working late nights to finish drawings and have them ready for my project manager the next morning. I'd hand him the final prints, he'd review them, and if they were good, he would say thanks and I'd move on to the next project or task.

If they still needed some work, I'd quickly turn that around for him. It was very transactional, but it was fun work, and I was good at my job. I wanted to learn as much as I could, but when I was let go, all my dreams were gone.

Or so I thought.

What's amazing to think is that through my architectural work at the firm, I still have my "fingerprint," so to speak, on nearly 100 buildings scattered throughout the United States. For some, I drew entire plans, while on others I did minor work. Nonetheless, they're out there—and nobody will ever know.

That is, unless you've been to the P.F. Chang's restaurant in Waikiki, Hawaii, which I always have to point out to my family when we're out there because I worked on that one. My kids roll their eyes each time I tell them that "P.F." actually stands for Pat Flynn.

After creating a new life, finding inspiration in online business and then learning how to teach others—first how to pass the LEED exam, and then all aspects of building an internet-based company—the work is now far from just transactional. It's life-changing and meaningful work for me. The ability to reach and teach others all over the world from a computer on my desk at home still feels incredibly profound, and it's morphed into a focus on nurturing a community that amplifies this impact, connecting like-minded individuals who support and inspire each other, turning individual success stories into a collective force for good.

Weeks after publishing my study guide for the LEED exam, I started receiving emails and letters from students who passed their tests. Some letters were lengthy and revealed how passing the exam helped them earn a promotion, a raise, or even helped families through some tough times. It was such an odd but amazing feeling to be personally thanked for those things, because I had never had that kind of praise before at my 9 to 5.

I had built buildings that people walk through every day, and even some that people call home. Yet, those people will never know I was a part of that story. However, in our own little corners of the internet, neighborhoods, and homes, we can teach others and have an immediate impact on another person's life. In return, we don't just get a thank-you, we get to grow while we teach, too. When you teach others, they can also teach you.

As you progress through your Lean Learning journey, a final step in the cycle to solidify what you've learned and achieve mastery is sharing your knowledge with others. As the saying goes, "the best way to learn is to teach" and that's true. By teaching others, you not only reinforce your own understanding of something but also create a powerful force function that drives you to deepen your knowledge and find ways to make complex concepts more accessible.

This book is a prime example of the transformative power of teaching. The process of writing has forced me to extract and articulate the concepts I've lived and practiced in a more thorough and intentional way. By committing to sharing my knowledge with you, I've gained a deeper understanding of the Lean Learning framework and discovered new insights and connections that I hadn't fully appreciated before.

Teaching others also opens up a world of opportunities for personal and professional growth. It allows you to establish yourself as a thought leader in your field and make a positive impact on the lives of others. Sharing your knowledge helps to build meaningful relationships—from the students you serve to the partners you collaborate with, many could potentially become lifelong friends.

When sharing happens, we create a ripple effect that extends far beyond our immediate circle of influence, and in my humble opinion, this is what we need more of in the world. When everybody shares, everybody wins.

In this chapter, we'll explore the many ways that you can build your own Lean Learning communities. These opportunities will allow you to demonstrate what you know, and learn even more along the way. We'll delve into the benefits of each approach, share precise strategies for implementation, and draw inspiration from real-world examples of individuals who have successfully leveraged these techniques to accelerate their learning, advance their careers, and create value for others.

The Power of Teaching

Teaching is one of the most effective ways to solidify your own learning and deepen your expertise. When you teach others, you're forced to break down complex concepts into more digestible pieces, identify gaps in your own understanding, and find new ways to communicate ideas effectively. This process of distillation and articulation helps you gain a more comprehensive grasp of the subject matter and uncover new insights and connections.

After I wrote my first study guide and started *The Smart Passive Income Blog*, I created a small PDF guide called *eBooks the Smart Way*, a step-by-step manual on how to write and launch your own eBook. Anyone could take their expertise, structure it into an eBook format, and either give it away to collect more email subscribers, or sell it directly on their website just like I did.

While creating that guide, I ended up creating a systematized approach that I could use to streamline my own book-writing processes. That led to publishing more books, faster, which helped me generate even more email subscribers, and more sales. I naturally learned a lot more by figuring out how to teach the concept to my audience.

More than that, the follow-up questions from my audience helped guide me even more. For example, after sharing *eBooks the Smart Way*, many people started to ask me questions I had never considered, like "how do I create a two-column eBook?" or "what's the best font size for someone reading on their computer?" These questions triggered research that helped me find answers that were extremely useful for me to know, and it was also very easy to add those updates to the eBook.

Readers who finished the guide and wrote their own eBooks came back to me and asked follow-up questions like "How do I set up my email list?," "How do I design a book cover?," and "How do I get my book on Amazon?" All these crowdsourced questions guided my personal learning journey even more.

As you engage with their unique challenges and viewpoints, you'll be pushed to think more critically about your own assumptions and blind spots. You'll learn to anticipate common obstacles and develop more nuanced approaches to problemsolving. This constant feedback loop between teacher and student creates a dynamic learning environment that benefits everyone involved.

So how can you start teaching others and reaping these benefits? Here are a few practical strategies I've used:

1. **Host a workshop or webinar.** Identify a specific skill or topic that you've mastered and develop a structured workshop or webinar to share your knowledge with others. This could be a one-time event or

an ongoing series, depending on your goals and audience. Be sure to create engaging content, include interactive elements like Q&A sessions or group exercises, and provide valuable takeaways that participants can apply in their own lives or work.

2. **Create a mini-course or tutorial.** If you have a particular expertise that lends itself to a more in-depth learning experience, consider creating an online course or tutorial. Platforms like Udemy, Skillshare, and Teachable make it easy to develop and distribute your content to a global audience. Break your course into manageable modules, include a mix of video, audio, and written content, and provide exercises and assessments to help students apply what they've learned.

3. **Write a blog or article series.** If you enjoy writing, consider starting a blog or contributing to publications in your field. Choose topics that align with your expertise and provide valuable insights and actionable advice for your readers. Consistency is key when building an audience, so aim to publish on a regular schedule and promote your content through social media and other channels.

4. **Speak at conferences or events.** Look for opportunities to share your knowledge and experience with others through speaking engagements. This could

include industry conferences, meetups, or even virtual events. Develop a compelling talk that showcases your unique perspective and offers takeaways for your audience. Be sure to engage with attendees before and after your talk to build relationships and expand your network.

5. **Find a friend or peer that needs help.** As we discussed in Chapter 3, our champions need us as much as we need them. Find a colleague or someone in your circles who may benefit from the knowledge and experience that you've gained on your journey, and share it. Schedule a time to meet on Zoom or in person, and it's up to you how detailed you want to be. It could simply be a casual conversation, or you could go all out, like my business partner Matt Gartland does when I have a question. He's the financial wizard in our partnership and knows a lot more about the back-end parts of a business than I do, so when I have a question about financial projections, operating agreements, or stock options, Matt usually finds a way to present a PowerPoint to me that helps both of us understand these concepts even more.

Also, teach your kids. Of course, not everyone has kids or cares to be around them, but if you do—or even if you don't—hear me out. When I teach my kids concepts that I learn about life and business, I have to break things down into their simplest forms so that they can understand. This was especially true when they were younger; however, even though they're both nearly teenagers now, I do forget how little experience they have in the world, and how important it is for me to teach things in a way that will resonate and stick with them.

This is an exercise in and of itself, but it also, at the same time, helps me bond with my kids and give them an understanding of the kinds of things I do as their father. It's also an opportunity for me to instill values that I hope stay with them for the rest of their lives.

Kids are curious, as we know, so until they grow out of curiosity like the rest of us have in our lives, I'm going to take advantage of that. My hope is, however, that through the teachings of Lean Learning, we'll all remain as curious as we once were as children and continue to lift each other up as humans.

Kids are great teachers, too, if you give them a chance. For the longest time, when my kids were younger and of elementary school age, instead of asking them how their day was, or "what did you do at school today?" I'd ask them, "What did you learn today that you can teach me?"

You could literally see their eyes light up, then a barrage of words would stream from their mouths. It was awesome. And of course, when given a chance to teach, they were solidifying their learning at the same time.

Work in Public

In addition to teaching others directly, another powerful way to demonstrate your learning and expertise is by sharing your skills and achievements in public, not because you want to show off, but because you deserve to display what you've accomplished, and the lessons you've been learning along the way. It's likely to inspire others, too.

Bryan Harris, who is the founder of the business coaching company Growth Tools, calls this "learning out loud"—and I love that. It's what so many of us did early on with blogging and podcasting. We weren't experts yet; we were just sharing what we were learning, because it helped us learn better. Teaching is the ultimate hack to becoming a better learner. What you teach, you learn better.

Plus, there are other benefits to learning out loud. When you make your work visible and share your process and insights with others, you not only establish your credibility and authority in your field, but you also create opportunities for feedback, collaboration, and growth. This kind of transparency invites others into the process, which will only help you improve faster.

When I think of working in public, Arvid Kahl comes to mind. Arvid is a successful developer and engineer, and he's openly sharing his journey, and all of the behind-the-scenes work that goes into developing an application called Podscan.fm, a clever tool any brand can use to create an alert every time the brand is mentioned on a podcast episode.

Arvid is building his software in real time, and it's fascinating to see it all unfold—the good, the bad, and the ugly. In addition to his audience holding him accountable to continue his work, as a member of his audience, we also get to enjoy the ride. We celebrate his wins together, like when he reported $500 in monthly recurring revenue. And at the same time, we feel the setbacks, like when he recently posted on social media: *"I spent all day today trying to wrangle a queue of millions of to-be-downloaded-and-transcribed podcast episodes into a manageable form. 9h in. Just got it done."*

We get to see Arvid figure things out, and we learn along the way with him. We're not just watching a drama or hero's journey unfold—we get to participate in the action, too. He recently posted a problem: *"I seem to have a memory leak in my code . . . only in the evenings. Every afternoon, my php-fpm pools start growing, requiring a restart every few minutes. I come back to it in the morning, and it's calm. There are no traffic spikes. Same throughput. Let the debugging begin."*

And his audience of developers immediately flew in to help troubleshoot with highly specific insights. By providing transparent insights into his process, challenges, and successes, he not only builds trust and credibility but also creates valuable opportunities for learning and growth—for himself and for everyone watching. This collaborative dynamic not only enhances the quality of his work but fosters a sense of community and shared investment in the project. The audience wants to see it succeed, and so far he's doing very well. Podscan.fm continues to grow and currently has over 11 million podcast episodes in its database.

Working in public also serves as a powerful marketing strategy for Arvid. By regularly sharing his progress and inviting his audience to participate in the journey, he generates organic buzz and anticipation around Podscan.fm. This authentic, real-time engagement is far more effective than traditional marketing tactics, as it allows potential users and stakeholders to witness the product's evolution firsthand and develop a genuine connection with the brand.

Arvid's commitment to transparency and collaboration is a testament to the value of working in public. By openly sharing his knowledge, experiences, and progress, he not only accelerates his own learning and growth but also inspires and empowers others in the developer community to do the same. His approach demonstrates that working in public is not just a means of building a successful product or company, but also a powerful way to create meaningful connections, drive innovation, and make a lasting impact in one's field.

Here are a few ways you can showcase your skills and attract new opportunities:

1. **Build a portfolio.** If you work in a creative or technical field, having a strong portfolio is essential for demonstrating your capabilities and attracting new clients or job opportunities. Choose your best work and present it in a visually compelling way, whether through a website, online platform, or physical book. Be sure to include detailed case studies that showcase your process, highlight the challenges you

faced and the solutions you developed, and demonstrate the impact of your work.

2. **Share your work on social media.** Social media platforms like LinkedIn, X, and Instagram are powerful tools for showcasing your skills and engaging with your professional community. Share updates on your projects, insights from your learning journey, and examples of your work. Engage with others in your field by commenting on their posts, asking questions, and participating in relevant discussions. Over time, you'll build a strong personal brand and establish yourself as an active and knowledgeable member of your industry. Plus, depending on the kind of work you do, you may end up booking more clients, getting more leads, and generating more revenue, too. Be sure to serve first, and let your earnings become a by-product of how well you serve your audience.

3. **Contribute to open-source projects.** If you're a developer or designer, contributing to open-source projects is a great way to showcase your skills and give back to your community. Look for projects that align with your interests and expertise, and start by fixing small bugs or adding minor features. As you gain more experience and confidence, take on larger challenges and collaborate with other contributors. Not only will you enhance your technical skills, but

you'll also build relationships with other professionals in your field and demonstrate your commitment to your craft.

Another reason I connect with Arvid's real-time build of Podscan.fm is because I took a similar approach to learning and working in public on *The Smart Passive Income Blog*. The reason this was important to me was because I didn't want to just tell people what to do. I wanted to show them. And by publishing regular updates about everything—from what businesses I was working on to exactly how much revenue I was generating—not only was I building trust through transparency, but I was journaling my journey and learning more quickly as I distilled that information for others.

For example, in 2010, with everyone watching over my shoulder, I publicly built a website from scratch to show people how it could be done. In a niche I knew nothing about—security guard training—I was able to build a website, do the proper research, and write blog posts to serve that audience.

After only seventy-three days, the website reached the #1 spot on Google for the search term "security guard training." When that happened, the story went viral, and because I had documented the entire process, thousands of people followed the same case study and were able to build websites of their own and generate revenue, as well, thanks to that work. I also included affiliate links, which allowed me to generate a commission from anyone who went through those links and purchased the same tools I used. I earned an additional $20,000 per month after that series of posts, and that revenue remained steady for over five years until niche website creation started to die off.

In 2020, I sold that security guard website, and it became one of the most important case studies that introduced me and my brand to the world.

Building a Learning Community

Finally, one of the most rewarding aspects of demonstrating your learning and expertise is the opportunity to build community and collaborate with others who share your passions and goals. When I wrote my previous book, *Superfans*, I knew the world was heading toward a place where people would be seeking more connection than ever. And here we are, in a time when community has become more vital than ever before.

At SPI Media, we recognized the power of community early on, prompting a transformative shift in our business model in 2022. We moved from a focus on individual courses to a community-centered approach, and this strategic pivot has not only tripled our course completion rates for our students, but also deepened our connection with members, fostering meaningful interactions within the community and a deeper support for our brand. Everybody wins.

The true magic happens, however, when we extend these virtual connections into the real world. Whether it's members meeting other members because they happen to live close to each other, or members flying out to conferences and meetups to meet in bigger groups with us, the in-person interactions are becoming a growing and important part of our community strategy.

Even through my Pokémon YouTube channel, *Deep Pocket Monster*, I've leaned into community, too. Every Monday night, I go live on YouTube in front of thousands of people who join me in the chatroom, watching a grown man open shiny cardboard with characters on them. Our membership, called the Gem Mint Club, gets access to special giveaways and even a private Discord channel where the community can connect and chat online together, and it's a space for members to show off the latest pickups that they're adding to their own collections.

Even though I'm fairly new to the community as a creator, I've been able to create a live, in-person event and experience called Card Party that brings together Pokémon fans, collectors, and their favorite creators, all in one spot.

Our inaugural event in 2023 in Anaheim, California, drew over 2,500 attendees, and by 2024 in Orlando, Florida, we nearly doubled that figure. I crafted this event to be something I would love to attend myself, a place where I could bring my family and where we could dive into the vibrant world of Pokémon together. Held in expansive conference centers with interconnected ballrooms, the setup encourages spontaneous encounters and deepens the community feel.

Attendees can meet their online friends, forge new bonds, meet and get a picture with their favorite Pokémon creator, and engage in activities like trading cards or participating in a Pokémon scavenger hunt. It's an environment where everyone, from young fans to seasoned collectors, can share their passion and create lasting memories. In 2025, we're planning two events in Tampa Bay and Seattle to accommodate the demand. As some attendees have already said, it's like camp, but for Pokémon nerds. I love that.

Online or offline, it doesn't matter what the community is centered around; hubs like this become safe spaces where members can converge, share insights, and collaborate on projects face-to-face. They're not just about networking; they're about building lasting relationships and a sense of belonging. Each event is designed to reinforce that sense of community, whether it's through workshops, collaborative sessions, or social gatherings. That's the power of a learning community.

In today's digital age, those who excel at creating and nurturing these safe, engaging spaces for their communities—spaces that bridge the gap between online interaction and real-world connections—will stand out as leaders. Whether it's spreading knowledge, fostering collaboration, or simply providing a sanctuary for like-minded individuals, fulfilling the innate human need for connection is fundamental. As we continue to innovate and host more of these events, we're not just building a community—we're crafting a movement that thrives on shared growth and mutual support.

Within our SPI Community, my team and I have witnessed the incredible power of community firsthand. Partnerships are being formed, mastermind groups are being created, and questions are being answered—not just by our team, but by fellow community members who are eager to support one another. It's a beautiful thing to behold. And at the same time, even though we created the community, our members are now teaching us so much.

A lot of the topics of discussion help us understand what else we can offer help and support for, and many of our members know much more about certain topics than we do.

One of our members, for example, Junaid Ahmed, has a brand called Home Studio Mastery, and he helps our other members, and our own team, learn more about how to set up a professional-looking video studio at home.

Another student, named MV Braverman, specializes in email deliverability. She can help ensure emails you send to a list of subscribers don't end up in people's spam folders. She's even helped us on our team achieve better results.

The collaborative efforts and exchange of valuable information that happen when a community is built is pure magic. It's not just a two-way connection. It's like a beehive—and *honey*, it's worth it. (Okay, the metaphor was much better than the pun, but you get the idea.)

While we use a tool called Circle (which we love) to host our community at SPI, it's important to remember that technology should never be a barrier to bringing people together. The key is to start small, learn from each other, and grow together over time.

By embracing the opportunity to build community and collaborate with others who share your passions and goals, you'll not only enhance your learning and growth but create a ripple effect of positive change that extends far beyond your immediate circle of influence.

So, take the time to cultivate meaningful connections, foster a spirit of collaboration, and watch as your impact and influence continue to grow in ways you never thought possible.

Here are a few ways you can build community and collaborate with others in your field:

1. **Join or create a mastermind group.** Look for existing groups in your industry or area of interest, or consider starting your own with a few trusted colleagues or friends. Set clear guidelines for participation, establish a regular meeting schedule, and create a supportive and challenging environment that encourages growth and collaboration. As I mentioned earlier in Chapter 3 when discussing champions, I've been a part of two groups that have met weekly for over ten years. One of the groups I joined was already running, and the other I just created with a friend.

2. **Participate in industry events and conferences.** Attending events and conferences in your field is a great way to meet other professionals, learn about new trends and best practices, and showcase your own expertise. Look for opportunities to volunteer, speak, or lead workshops, and be sure to engage with other attendees and speakers throughout the event. Follow up with new connections after the event to continue building relationships and exploring opportunities for collaboration. Ask your colleagues and peers what events they attend and recommend, and be sure to go into these events with goals in mind, for example specific people that you'd like

to meet, companies you'd like to collaborate with, and Just-in-Time Information that you'd like to take home and implement. Also be aware of the online events that happen in your space, too!

3. **Contribute to industry publications and blogs.** Writing for industry publications and blogs is a powerful way to share your knowledge and insights with a wider audience and establish yourself as a thought leader in your field. Look for publications that align with your expertise and target audience, and pitch article ideas that provide value and showcase your unique perspective. Be sure to promote your published work through your own channels and engage with readers who comment on or share your articles.

4. **Collaborate on a project or initiative.** Finally, consider collaborating with others in your field on a specific project or initiative that aligns with your shared goals and values. This could be anything from coauthoring a book or research paper to launching a new product or service. Look for partners who complement your skills and experience, and establish clear roles, responsibilities, and expectations from the outset. Embrace the challenges and opportunities that come with collaboration, and celebrate your shared successes along the way.

Embrace the Learning-Teaching Cycle

Demonstrating your learning and expertise is not only a powerful way to reinforce your own understanding and skills. It's also an incredible opportunity to create value for others and build meaningful relationships and collaborations. By embracing the learning-teaching cycle, you'll unlock a virtuous feedback loop that fuels your growth and impact over time.

Of course, taking the leap from learning to leading can be daunting at first. You may feel like you're not ready or that you don't have anything valuable to share. But remember that everyone starts somewhere, and your unique perspective and experiences are valuable in their own right. Start small, focus on providing value to others, and trust in the power of the Lean Learning framework to guide you.

To many, an expert can be someone who is just a couple steps ahead, so remember that no matter where you're at, there are others behind you that you can serve and help along the way.

As you take action and share your knowledge with the world, try to approach every opportunity as a chance to learn. Embrace feedback and criticism as gifts to help you refine your skills and understanding. Celebrate your successes and failures as essential steps on the path to mastery. And above all, stay curious, stay humble, and stay committed to the lifelong journey of learning and leading.

In the words of Maya Angelou, "When you learn, teach. When you get, give." By embracing this philosophy and putting it into practice every day, you'll not only accelerate your own learning and growth but create a ripple effect of change that extends far beyond your own life and work. So go forth and share your gifts with the world, friend. The journey ahead starts with a step, and your next move begins now.

Conclusion

You Know Enough to Begin

"The beginning is the most important part of the work."

—Plato

Several years ago, a reader of mine named Pamela Acosta decided to take part in the reenactment of an ancient Mayan pilgrimage—a canoe ride starting in mainland Mexico and continuing to the island of Cozumel. The goal of the pilgrimage is to honor Ix-Chel, the Mayan goddess of the moon, fertility, and childbirth. The journey traverses approximately thirty-six kilometers (around twenty-two miles) across the open sea. It is an event organized by a private theme park in the Riviera Maya as a way to keep indigenous traditions alive. Most participants train for at least six months to embark on the journey.

While working at the park as a content creator and community manager, Pam, originally from Ontario, witnessed the magic of the event firsthand. She saw how profoundly it affected participants and couldn't help but feel like the pilgrimage was calling to her. So in 2013, when posters with the invitation to sign up were plastered all over the halls of her workplace, she could no longer ignore the nudge.

Pam signed up.

There was just one problem: she didn't know how to swim. Assuming the process would be gradual and there'd be plenty of time to learn to swim before she tackled the Mayan ritual that summer, Pam jumped in, so to speak, headfirst. A friend had told her Ix-Chel and the sea were beckoning her, and she believed that. But it would be crazy to sign up for a daylong canoe trip out into the ocean without knowing how to swim.

So her next step was obvious: Pam signed up for swimming lessons. She figured she wouldn't actually get in the water until they were deep into the training, but she was wrong. On the first day of preparation, at 6 a.m., an Uruguayan, military-trained coach yelled at the over 100 half-asleep humans to get into the water and swim a lap.

At this point, Pam had two choices: she could either grab her things, get on a bus, and go home to Canada, or she could get in the water and hope what little swimming she *did* know would be enough. She chose the latter.

The following May, while dressed in traditional Mayan clothing, Pam, along with over 300 other intrepid souls, rowed for four hours from Xcaret to Cozumel to participate in the pilgrimage, culminating in a presentation of offerings to the goddess. To this day, she considers this one of the best experiences in her life. She doesn't regret pushing through her discomfort, doesn't regret putting herself out there and figuring out the rest. What she found on the other side of her fear—on the other side of that pilgrimage—was a sense of confidence and strength that cannot be taken away from her.

This is the power of Lean Learning. It can change your life if you let it.

The lesson here, of course, isn't to put yourself in harm's way. There were people around Pam who would have helped her if she got into serious trouble. She had her champions all right. And although she'd done minimal training ahead of time, Pam did put in the hours to get her Just-in-Time Training so that she was as ready as she could be.

She also implemented the power of the Keystone Question—"If this were easy, what would it look like?"—and made the most of her limited window, training every day, readying herself for the journey.

Signing up for the pilgrimage in spite of not feeling fully ready was Pam's Voluntary Force Function and in her training she employed her own Power 10, pushing hard for the months leading up to the voyage.

In that time, she saw a Quantum Leap forward in what she believed she was capable of. And even though on the day of the ceremony she still did not feel fully ready, Pam did it, anyway. She took bold, brave action. And it worked.

Of course it worked. Lean Learning is not complicated, but it does require effort and intentionality—not only that, it requires commitment.

The truth is we are never ready for the challenges that await us, but if we choose to follow Pam's example and become Lean Learners, we can make the most of our opportunities, however imperfect they may be.

Or, we can choose the path of the content hoarder and keep

acquiring new information, continuing to wait for the right opportunity or better resources, and wonder why we aren't seeing any results.

You and I have an opportunity here. We can start changing our lives and everything in them today by doing something different now—or we can wait. We can delay.

We can choose to believe we know enough to begin, or we can hold off until we feel more prepared. We can get in the water, or we can stand on the shore. It's just that simple, and it's up to us: to you, and to me.

The Power of Lean Learning in a Rapidly Changing World

It's clear that the traditional educational models that have served us for decades are now struggling to keep up with the rapid advancements in technology, the shifting demands of business, and the ever-changing needs of most people. In this new and changing landscape, the ability to adapt, learn quickly, and remain useful is more crucial than ever.

Throughout this book, we've explored the power of Lean Learning—a methodology that empowers us to acquire new skills, solve problems, and navigate the complexities of the modern world with greater agility and efficiency. By focusing on the right problems, seeking out the essential information, and taking bold action, we can accelerate our growth, unlock new opportunities, and create meaningful impact in our personal and professional lives.

As we've seen, Lean Learning is not just a set of strategies or techniques, but a fundamentally different approach to learning and growth. It challenges us to let go of the notion that we need to know everything before we can begin and instead encourages us to embrace the power of incremental progress, continuous improvement, and the willingness to learn as we go.

In a world where artificial intelligence and automation are transforming entire industries and redefining the nature of work, the ability to learn quickly and adapt to new challenges has become a critical competitive advantage. By embracing the principles in this book, you can position yourself to thrive in a rapidly evolving landscape—developing the skills, knowledge, and mindset needed to stay relevant, valuable, and impactful for years to come.

But Lean Learning is not just about acquiring new skills or getting a better job. It's also about unlocking your full potential as a human being, pursuing your passion, and making a positive difference in the world. When you approach learning with a spirit of curiosity, humility, and a willingness to take action, you open yourself up to a world of possibility and opportunity.

In this book, we've explored the key components of the Lean Learning framework, from identifying the right problems to solve and gathering Just-in-Time Information to leveraging the power of mentors and communities and more. We've seen how Micro Mastery and taking bold actions can accelerate our progress and how teaching others and working in public can deepen our understanding and amplify our impact. But perhaps the most powerful lesson of all is that Lean Learning is not just a destination but a lifelong journey of growth, discovery, and transformation. It's a pilgrimage of sorts that requires us to embrace discomfort, challenge our assumptions, and push beyond our limitations. It's a journey that demands courage, resilience, and a willingness to take risks and learn from our failures.

And yet, as we've seen through the inspiring stories and examples in this book, the rewards of Lean Learning are immeasurable. From Ori's journey of artistic rediscovery and Brian's bold pivot into entrepreneurship, to Nathan's leap of faith with ConvertKit and Pam's transformative canoe trip, these stories remind us of what we are capable of.

Pam's story, in particular, serves as a reminder that we are never truly ready for the challenges and opportunities awaiting us. But by choosing to take the first step, to just get in the water and figure it out, we set in motion a chain of events that can transform our lives in ways we never would have otherwise imagined. Likewise, as you reflect on your own life, I encourage you to embrace the power of Lean Learning.

Start by identifying the problems and challenges that matter most to you, then take bold action to begin solving them. Seek out essential information and resources you need, but don't get bogged down in the pursuit of perfection. Instead, focus on incremental progress, learning from your mistakes, and celebrating your successes. And don't forget that you don't have to do this alone. Surround yourself with those who will champion you: mentors, peers, a community of like-minded individuals who will cheer you on, challenge you, and help you grow into who you could become. Then, to complete the cycle, embrace the power of teaching others as you go, and watch as your impact and influence expand in surprising and helpful ways.

Above all, remember that Lean Learning is not about reaching a destination or achieving a specific goal. It's about embracing a mindset of continuous growth, curiosity, and adaptability. Really, this is all about loving the learning journey, with all its ups and downs, twists and turns, and unexpected detours. So as you embark on your own journey, remember to stay curious, humble, and committed to the process. Most importantly, remember that you have everything you need to succeed, thrive, and make a positive impact.

In the words of the philosopher Lao Tzu, "The journey of a thousand miles begins with a single step." So take that first step today, trusting in the power of Lean Learning to guide you on this transformative path of growth and discovery.

And as we close the pages of this book, I leave you with a final challenge and invitation. Take a moment to reflect on the problems and challenges that matter most to you, the skills and knowledge you want to acquire, and the impact you want to make. Then, choose one small action you can take today. Just to get started. It might be reaching out to a mentor, signing up for a course, or setting aside some time to reflect on your priorities. Whatever it is, make a commitment to yourself to take that first step, then keep taking the next step, day after day, week after week, and month after month.

Remember, the power of this process lies in small, daily actions that compound over time. So embrace the small steps and the simple starts. And as you go forth and apply these principles and strategies, know that you are part of a growing community of individuals and teams committed to learning, growth, and making a positive impact. Together, we have the power to transform ourselves, our communities, and the world around us, one small step at a time.

Resources

Lean Learning Companion Course

To get the most out of this book, I invite you to get access to the *Lean Leaning* bonus companion course, a free chapter-by-chapter online course with supplemental material that may be useful for you as you read through (and more importantly, take action with) this book. Here, you'll find PDF downloads, videos, and other bonus materials to enhance your lean learning experience!

Please visit the following link to get free access to your *Lean Learning* companion course now and I'll see you inside!
leanlearningbook.com/course

You're invited to Join the SPI Community

If you're an entrepreneur or looking to start a business of your own soon, it's important to surround yourself with like-minded people who are going through the same journey. It's also important to get access to the right information from the right people. Join thousands of other students who are learning the smart way, using lean learning principles, to start an online business inside of the SPI Community! With access to online courses, live events, and community support, you'll be setting yourself up for success and be able to find the champions who can help you get there. From finding an idea to scaling up and generating revenue, the SPI community is the premier community for online business education.

Please visit the following link to see how you can get started: smartpassiveincome.com/community

Acknowledgments

This book is not just a product of my efforts but the culmination of support and inspiration from a host of champions in both my personal and professional life.

First and foremost, to my gorgeous wife, April, and my amazing kids, Keoni and Kailani—your patience and encouragement have been my anchor and beacon throughout the intense process of writing this book. Each day, you inspire me to pursue my passions and strive for excellence. You are my greatest champions.

I am profoundly grateful to my publisher, Stephanie Hitchcock, and the incredible team at Simon Acumen and Simon & Schuster. Your belief in my vision transformed this journey into an extraordinary experience. Your guidance was more than professional; it was a mentorship that enriched both the pages of this book and my personal growth.

A heartfelt thank you to my literary agent, Christy Fletcher. Your enthusiasm for this project sparked excitement at every turn. I am truly your superfan for all the energy and belief you've poured into this work.

Acknowledgments

To my business partner, Matt Gartland, and the rest of the incredible team at SPI—thank you for weathering the storms and celebrations during the writing of this book. Your steadfast support never wavered one bit. And Jess Lindgren, my business manager, your organizational skills and sanity checks were indispensable. I couldn't have navigated this process without you.

A special thanks to Jeff Goins, not only for your collaboration during the writing process but for helping sculpt my thoughts into the final product that graces these pages. And to Chantel Goins, whose keen insights helped refine and beautify this work.

To my mastermind group members—Mark Mason, Michael Stelzner, Cliff Ravenscraft, Leslie Samuel, Ray Edwards, Jaime Masters, Shawn Stevenson, Rosemarie Groner, and Todd Tressider—thank you for being the sounding board and pillars of support from the inception of the Lean Learning idea. Your guidance through the toughest decisions and your cheers toward the finish line were instrumental in bringing this project to fruition. Your commitment to our shared journey is invaluable, and I am deeply grateful for each of you.

To my mentors and dear friends—Michael Hyatt, Amy Porterfield, James Schramko, Chris Ducker, Rick Mulready, Caleb Wojcik, Azul Terronez, Jay Papasan, Donald Miller, Mike Michalowicz, Rory Vaden—your wisdom has been a guiding light. Your mentorship and friendship have been invaluable and are deeply cherished.

This journey has been supported by countless individuals, each of whom deserves their own story of recognition—so many, in fact, that it could fill another book. Writing this book has been a profound challenge and a deeply rewarding experience. It has reinforced not only the principles of Lean Learning but the incredible strength that lies in a community of supporters and believers.

To everyone who has been part of this adventure—my champions—thank you from the bottom of my heart. Your support has not just propelled this book into existence; it has enriched my life immeasurably.

Notes

Introduction: You Know Too Much

1. Haiyang Ding, Bing Cao, and Qixuan Sun, "The Association Between Problematic Internet Use and Social Anxiety Within Adolescents and Young Adults: A Systematic Review and Meta-analysis" (*Frontiers in Public Health* 11: September 29, 2023), https://doi.org/10.3389/fpubh.2023.1275723.

Chapter 1: Inspiration Overload and the Art of Selective Curiosity

1. Richard Wiseman. "New Year's Resolution Project" (*Quirkology*), http://www.richardwiseman.com/quirkology /new/USA/Experiment_resolution.shtml.

Chapter 2: Choosing Action over Information

1. Amy Edmondson, "It's OK to Fail, but You Have to Do It Right" (*Harvard Business Review*, July 28, 2023), https://hbr.org/2023/07/its-ok-to-fail-but-you-have-to-do-it-right.

Chapter 4: Protect Your Progress

1. Daniel Kahneman, *Thinking, Fast and Slow* (New York: Farrar, Straus & Giroux, 2011), 24.

Chapter 5: Voluntary Force Functions

1. Peter M. Gollwitzer and Paschal Sheeran, "Implementation Intentions and Goal Achievement: A Meta-analysis of Effects and Processes," in *Advances in Experimental Social Psychology*, (2206), 69–119, https://doi.org/10.1016/s0065-2601(06)38002-1.
2. Grabmeier, Jeff. "Share Your Goals—But Be Careful Whom You Tell," Ohio State University, September 10, 2019, https://news.osu.edu/share-your-goals--but-be-careful-whom-you-tell.

Chapter 6: Persist or Pivot?

1. Mihaly Csikszentmihalyi, *Flow: The Psychology of Optimal Experience* (New York: Harper & Row, 1990).

Index

Index

in Voluntary Force Function, 93,
102–103
to wrong path, 24–25
communities
building, 51–55, 186–191
of champions, 51–55
in Lean Learning framework,
199–201
learning, 186–191
of peer champions, 61–63
rekindling your passion in, 128
seeking feedback from, 136–137
complex failures, 39
compounding effects of Micro
Mastery, 149–154
conferences, 178–179, 190–191
confidence, 95, 112, 196
consensus building, xiv
constructive criticism, 138–139
ConsultaBlindGuy.com, 22
content creators
bold move of reaching out to,
170–171
as virtual mentors, 63–64
continual improvement, 145
continuous learning, 41–42
conversion rate, improving,
151–154
ConvertKit, 158–161, 200
Cooper, Alice, 144
Copperfield, David, 144
core values
opportunities aligned with, 90–92
passion and alignment with, 129
and personal mission statement,
134, 135
and personal why, 116–117

Voluntary Force Functions that
align with, 105
Corica Park Golf Course (Alameda,
Calif.), 70
courage, to make bold moves,
170–172
Covid pandemic, 44–45
"crabs in a bucket" mentality, 85
Crazy Egg, 159
Critical Commitments, on
Inspiration Matrix, 9, 16–17
criticism, 84–88, 138–139, 192
CrossFit gyms, 61
crossroads, decision-making at, *see*
persist or pivot decision
Csikszentmihalyi, Mihaly, 130
curiosity
approaching feedback with, 139
approaching new skills with,
125–127
inspiration and, 29
in lean Learning framework, 201
in learning-teaching cycle, 180,
192, 199
mistakes that stimulate, 41
Passion Pursuits that start as, 12
selective, xxiv, xxix
without boundaries, 3

D

deadlines, 102–103
Deep Pocket Monster (YouTube
channel), 36, 187
Deep Work (Newport), 79
delegation, 127–128
deliverability, 152–153, 189
detail, attention to, 155

213

Index

Index

Jeopardy! (TV series), xx

JITI, *see* Just-in-Time Information

job loss

    anti-champions after, 84–85

    champions after, 57

    embracing opportunities after, 46

    necessity-driven inspiration after,
      5–6

    pivoting after, 113–114

job opportunities, thought
    experiment to explore, 22–23

joy of opting out, 90–92

Junk Sparks, 9, 13–16, 20

Just-in-Time Information (JITI), 73–77

    from industry events and
      conferences, 191

    in Lean Learning framework, 74,
      199

    Micro Mastery using, 151, 152, 156

    in Voluntary Force Functions, 98

K

Kahl, Arvid, 181–183, 185

Kahneman, Daniel, 82

Keller, Helen, 51

Kerouac, Jack, 166

Kickstarter, 35

King, Regina, 158

KISSmetrics, 159

Kit (formerly ConvertKit), 160

Klein, Howard, 110

Knighton, Boots, 130

KovaaK's (video game), 149

L

language, learning a new, 102, 108

Lao Tzu, 201

Lean Learning

    author's use of, xix

    being ready to apply, 195–198

    defined, xix

    efficiency of, xxiv

    importance of, xxvi–xxix

    mindset for, xxvii–xxviii, 201

    in rapidly changing world,
      198–202

    steps in, xxiii

    see also specific components

LeanLearningBook.com, 58, 112, 203

Lean Startup, The (Ries), 139

Leap of Faith Moment, 101–102, 111

learning

    continuous, 41–42

    perpetual, 46

    from practice, 71, 72

    scheduled, 79

    by sharing learning, 192–193

    trial-and-error approach to, xviii

learning communities, 186–191

learning curve, 7, 125

learning out loud, 181

learning-teaching cycle, 174–175,
    192–193

LEED AP Walkthrough Study Guide
    (Flynn), 76

LEED exam business

    asking for help in, 56

    eBook on passing LEED exam,
      32–33

    Just-in-Time Information in,
      75–77

    meaningful work in, 174

    mistake in naming, 42–43

LinkedIn, 184

Index

About the Author

Pat Flynn is a father, husband, and lifelong learner from San Diego who has built a reputation as one of the most influential voices in digital entrepreneurship. Through his diverse portfolio of businesses, award-winning podcasts, newsletters, YouTube channels, and thriving online communities, Pat reaches and inspires millions of people each month. He is the founder of SPI, an online community for digital entrepreneurs, coinventor of the SwitchPod, and host of the Deep Pocket Monster YouTube channel as well as founder of Card Party, a large-scale live event for the community of Pokémon collectors. Pat also serves as an advisor to dozens of companies and is a sought-after keynote speaker. In his free time, he enjoys fishing, collecting Pokémon cards, and rewatching the *Back to the Future* trilogy.